Fodor's 94 Pocket London

D0655038

Reprinted from *Fodor's London '94*.

Fodor's Travel Publications, Inc.
New York • Toronto • London •
Sydney • Auckland

Copyright © 1993
by Fodor's Travel Publications, Inc.

ISBN 0–679–02538–3

Fodor's Pocket London

Editors: Craig Seligman and Katherine Kane
Area Editor: Kate Sekules
Editorial Contributors: John Elsom, John Lahr,
Mark Lewes, Christopher Pick, Marcy Pritchard,
Ann Saunders
Creative Director: Fabrizio La Rocca
Cartographer: David Lindroth
Illustrator: Karl Tanner
Cover Photograph: Terry Williams/Image Bank

Design: Vignelli Associates

Special Sales

Contents

Maps

Foreword

While every care has been taken to ensure the accuracy of the information in this guide, the passage of time will always bring change, and consequently, the publisher cannot accept responsibility for errors that may occur.

All prices and opening times quoted here are based on information supplied to us at press time. Hours and admission fees may change, however, and the prudent traveler will avoid inconvenience by calling ahead.

Fodor's wants to hear about your travel experiences, both pleasant and unpleasant. When a hotel or restaurant fails to live up to its billing, let us know and we will investigate the complaint and revise our entries where the facts warrant it.

Send your letters to the editors of Fodor's Travel Publications, 201 E. 50th Street, New York, NY 10022.

Central London Exploring *(Boxes Refer to Detail Maps)*

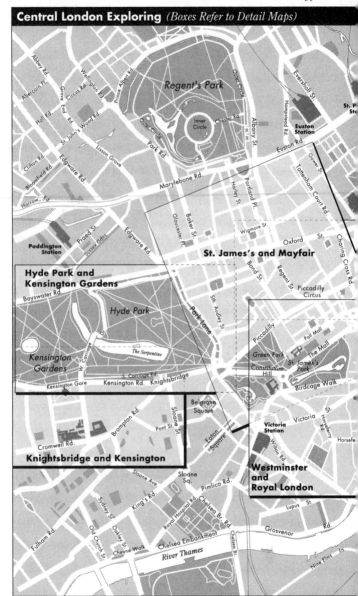

Abbey Rd.
Abercorn Pl.
Hall Rd.
Grove End Rd.
Circus Rd.
Wellington Rd.
Prince Albert Rd.
Outer Circle
Clifton Rd.
Bloomfield Rd.
Edgware Rd.
St. John's Wood Rd.
Lisson Grove
Harrow Rd.

Regent's Park

Inner Circle
Chester Rd.
Albany St.
Hampstead Rd.
Eversholt St.

St. P
Ste

Euston Station
Gower St.
Euston Rd.

Park Rd.
Marylebone Rd.

Paddington Station
Praed St.
Sussex Gdns.
Edgware Rd.

Baker St.
Gloucester Pl.
Harley St.
Portland Pl.
Wigmore St.
Tottenham Court Rd.
Charing Cross Rd.

St. James's and Mayfair

Oxford St.
Bond St.
Regent St.
Piccadilly Circus

Hyde Park and Kensington Gardens

Bayswater Rd.

Hyde Park

The Serpentine

Kensington Gardens

W. Carriage Dr.
S. Carriage Rd.
Kensington Gore
Kensington Rd.
Knightsbridge

Sth. Audley St.
Park Lane

Piccadilly
Pall Mall
The Mall
Green Park
Constitution Hill
St. James's Park
Birdcage Walk

Brompton Rd.
Pont St.
Sloane St.

Belgrave Square

Eaton Square

Victoria Station
Victoria St.
Horseferry Rd.
Wilton Rd.
Horsefe

Knightsbridge and Kensington

Cromwell Rd.

Sloane Ave.
Sloane Sq.
King's Rd.
Pimlico Rd.

Westminster and Royal London

Fulham Rd.
Sydney St.
Old Church St.
Oakley St.
Cheyne Walk

Royal Hospital Rd.
Chelsea Br. Rd.
Chelsea Embankment
Chelsea Br.

Lupus St.
Grosvenor Rd.
Nine Elms Ln.

River Thames

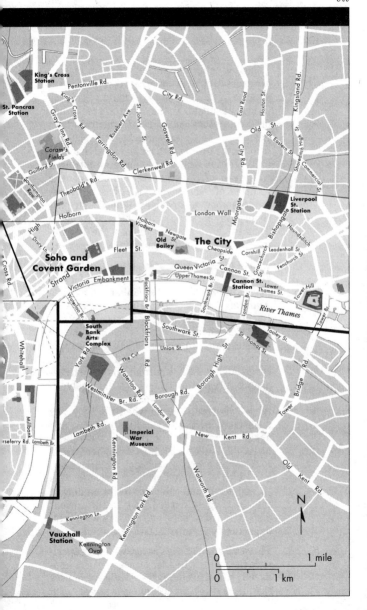

King's Cross Station

St. Pancras Station

Pentonville Rd.

City Rd.

East Road

Hoxton St.

Kingsland Rd.

King's Cross Rd.

Gray's Inn Rd.

St. John's St.

Goswell Rd.

Old St.

City Rd.

Gt. Eastern St.

Shoreditch High St.

Commercial St.

Coram's Fields

Guilford St.

Rosebery Ave.

Farringdon Rd.

Clerkenwell Rd.

Southampton Row

Theobald's Rd.

Holborn

London Wall

Moorgate

Bishopsgate

Liverpool St. Station

Houndsditch

High

Drury Ln.

Holborn Viaduct

Newgate St.

Old Bailey

The City

Cheapside

Cornhill

Leadenhall St.

Fenchurch St.

Fleet St.

Soho and Covent Garden

Strand

Queen Victoria St.

UpperThames St.

Cannon St.

Gracechurch St.

Lower Thames St.

Tower Hill

Cross Rd.

Victoria Embankment

Waterloo Br.

Blackfriars Br.

Cannon St. Station

River Thames

London Br.

Tower Br.

Whitehall

South Bank Arts Complex

York Rd.

Blackfriars Rd.

Southwark St.

Southwark Br.

Tooley St.

St. Thomas St.

Union St.

The Cut

Westminster Br. Rd.

Waterloo Rd.

Borough Rd.

Borough High St.

Tower Bridge Rd.

Millbank

rseferry Rd.

Lambeth Br.

Lambeth Rd.

Kennington Rd.

Kennington Park Rd.

London Rd.

New Kent Rd.

Walworth Rd.

Old Kent Rd.

Imperial War Museum

N

Kennington Ln.

Vauxhall Station

Kennington Oval

| 0 | | 1 mile |

| 0 | | 1 km |

Introduction

L ondon is an ancient city and its history greets you at every street corner. To gain a sense of its continuity, stand on Waterloo Bridge at sunset. To the east, the great globe of 17th-century St. Paul's Cathedral glows golden in the dying sunlight, still majestic despite the towers of glass and steel that hem it in. To the west stand the mock-medieval ramparts of Westminster, home of the "Mother of Parliaments" that has met here, or here-abouts, since the 1250s. And past them both snake the swift, dark waters of the Thames, flowing as they did past the first Roman settlement here nearly 2,000 years ago.

Unlike most European capitals, London has almost no grand boulevards, planned for display. The exception is the Mall, running from Admiralty Arch on Trafalgar Square to Buckingham Palace. It was specifically designed for heraldic processions and stately occasions and, in a typically British way, is surrounded by gardens and lined with spreading trees. Apart from this one extravagance, present-day London still largely reflects its medieval layout, a bewildering tangle of streets. Even when the City was devastated in the Great Fire of 1666, and again in the Blitz of the 1940s, it was rebuilt on its old street plan. Sir Christopher Wren's 17th-century master concept for a classical site, with vistas and crossing avenues, was turned down; and the plans for rebuilding in the 1950s again harked back to the ancient disposition of streets, and so lost a wonderful opportunity for imaginative replanning.

This is all gain for the visitor, who can experience the historic London atmosphere by wandering the thoroughfares of stately houses that lie next to a muddle of mean streets, and by seeking out the winding lanes and narrow courts that suddenly give onto the grass, trees, and flower beds of well-kept squares. These contrasts can best be savored as you walk from one neighborhood to another.

The key to London is thus a simple one. Explore for yourself off the beaten track. Use your feet, and when you are tired, take to the bus or the Underground. And look around you, for London's centuries of history and its vibrant daily life are revealed as much in the individual streets and houses of the city as in its grand national monuments and galleries.

Close-up exploration, however, will reveal that London, like all great cities, has its darker side: squalor and crowds are as much a part of every modern city as they were of medieval ones. Squalor will be near at hand as you stand on Waterloo Bridge.

On an icy winter's evening, when you are coming out of the warm Queen Elizabeth Hall at the southern end of the bridge after a concert, you will pass down-and-outs sheltering in cardboard lean-tos in the open spaces underneath the building, grateful for the mobile soup kitchen that rolls up every night at 10:30. Both Shakespeare and Dickens would have recognized the scene. Where crowds are concerned, London definitely has the edge on any city in Western Europe. It starts with the largest population—nearly 7 million live here—and has well over the same number of visitors every year. Indeed, in one busy year the tourists numbered 12 million!

Traditionally, London has been divided between the City (capital "C"), to the east, site of the original Roman settlement of Londinium, where its banking and commercial interests lie, and Westminster to the west, the seat of the royal court and of government. Today the distinction between the two holds good, and even the briefest exploration will demonstrate that each enjoys a quite distinct atmosphere. It is in these two areas also that you will find most of the grand buildings that have played a central role in British history: the Tower of London and St. Paul's Cathedral, Westminster Abbey and the Houses of Parliament, Buckingham Palace and the older royal palace of St. James's.

These sites are natural magnets for visitors to London, as the crowds of people and the ubiquitous tourist coaches demonstrate. But visitors who restrict their sightseeing to these well-known tourist traps miss much of the best the city has to offer. Within a few minutes' walk of Buckingham Palace, for instance, lie St. James's and Mayfair, two neighboring quarters of elegant town houses built for the nobility in the 17th and early 18th centuries, and now full of stylish shops patronized by an international, jet-setting clientele. The same lesson applies to the City, where, tucked away in quiet corners, stand many of the churches Christopher Wren built to replace those destroyed during the Great Fire of 1666.

Covent Garden, a former fruit and flower market, has been converted into a lively shopping and entertainment center with a bazaar where craftspeople sell their own wares. The atmosphere here is informal, and you can stroll for hours enjoying the friendly bustle of the streets. Hyde Park and Kensington Gardens, by contrast, offer a great swath of green parkland across the city center, preserved by past kings and queens for their own hunting and relaxation. A walk across Hyde Park will bring you to the museum district of South Kensington: the Natural History Museum, the Science Museum, and the Victoria and Albert Museum, which specializes in costume and the fine and applied arts.

1 Essential Information

Before You Go

Government Tourist Offices

Contact the **British Tourist Authority** for information.

In the United States 551 Fifth Ave., New York, NY 10036, tel. 212/986–2200; Suite 1510, 625 N. Michigan Ave., Chicago, IL 60611, tel. 312/787–0490; World Trade Center, 350 S. Figueroa St., Suite 450, Los Angeles, CA 90071, tel. 213/628–3525; 2580 Cumberland Pkwy., Suite 470, Atlanta, GA 30339, tel. 404/432–9635.

In Canada 111 Avenue Rd., 4th floor, Toronto, Ont. M5R 3J8, tel. 416/925–6326.

When to Go

The heaviest tourist season in Britain runs from mid-April to mid-October, with a small peak around Christmas—though the tide never really ebbs away. The spring is the time to see the countryside and the London gardens at their freshest; early summer to catch the roses and full garden splendor; the fall for near-ideal exploring conditions. The British take their vacations mainly in July and August, and the resorts are crowded. London in summer, however, though full of visitors, is also full of interesting things to see and do. But be warned: Air-conditioning is *very* rare in London, and in a hot summer you'll swelter. The winter can be rather dismal and is frequently wet and usually cold, but all the theaters, concerts, and exhibitions are going full speed.

Climate London's weather has always been contrary, and in recent years it has become positively erratic, with hot summers and mild winters proving the greenhouse effect is running rampant over Britain. It is virtually impossible to forecast what the pattern might be, but you can be fairly certain that it will not be what you expect! The main feature of the British weather is that it is generally mild—with some savage exceptions, especially in summer. It is also fairly damp—though even that has been changing in recent years with recurring periods of drought.

What follows are the average daily maximum and minimum temperatures for London.

Jan.	43F	6C	May	62F	17C	Sept.	65F	19C
	36	2		47	8		52	11
Feb.	44F	7C	June	69F	20C	Oct.	58F	14C
	36	2		53	12		46	8
Mar.	50F	10C	July	71F	22C	Nov.	50F	10C
	38	3		56	14		42	5
Apr.	56F	13C	Aug.	71F	21C	Dec.	45F	7C
	42	6		56	13		38	4

Information Sources For current weather conditions for cities in the United States and abroad, plus the local time and helpful travel tips, call the **Weather Channel Connection** (tel. 900/WEATHER; 95¢ per minute) from a touch-tone phone.

What to Pack

Clothing You'll need an overcoat for winter and a light coat or warm jacket for summer, and there's rarely a time of year when a raincoat or an umbrella won't come in handy. As in any American city, jackets and ties are appropriate for expensive restaurants and night spots; casual clothes are fine elsewhere. Jeans are as popular in Great Britain as they are at home and are perfectly acceptable for sightseeing and informal dining. Tweeds and nonmatching jackets are popular here with men. For women, ordinary street dress is acceptable everywhere.

Miscellaneous If you have a health problem that may require you to purchase a prescription drug, take enough to last the duration of the trip or have your doctor write a prescription using the drug's generic name, as brand names vary widely from country to country. If you plan to stay in budget hotels, take your own soap. And don't forget to pack a list of the addresses of offices that supply refunds for lost or stolen traveler's checks.

Electricity The electrical current in London is 220 volts, 50 cycles alternating current (AC); the United States runs on 110-volt, 60-cycle AC current. To plug in U.S.-made appliances, you'll need an adapter plug. To reduce the voltage entering the appliance from 220 to 110 volts, you'll also need a converter, unless it is a dual-voltage appliance, made for travel.

British Currency

The units of currency in Great Britain are pound sterling (£) and pence (p): £50, £20, £10, and £5 bills; £1 (100p), 50p, 20p, 10p, 5p, 2p, and 1p coins. At press time, the exchange rate was about $1.62 U.S. dollars, or $1.96 Canadian dollars, to the British pound.

Passports and Visas

If your passport is lost or stolen abroad, report it immediately to the nearest embassy or consulate and to the local police. If you can provide the consular officer with the information contained in the passport, they will usually be able to issue you a new passport. For this reason, it is a good idea to keep a copy of the data page of your passport in a separate place, or to leave the passport number, date, and place of issuance with a relative or friend at home.

U.S. Citizens All U.S. citizens, even infants, need a valid passport to enter Great Britain for stays of up to six months.

You can pick up new and renewal application forms at any of the 13 U.S. Passport Agency offices and at some post offices and courthouses. Although passports are usually mailed within two weeks of your application's receipt, it's best to allow three weeks for delivery in low season, five weeks or more from April through summer. Call the Department of State Office of Passport Services' information line (1425 K St. NW, Washington, DC 20522, tel. 202/647–0518) for details.

Canadian Citizens Canadian citizens need a valid passport to enter Great Britain for stays of up to six months.

Application forms are available at 23 regional passport offices as well as at post offices and travel agencies. Whether applying for a first or subsequent passport, you must apply in person. Children under 16 may be included on a parent's passport but must have their own passport to travel alone. Passports are valid for five years and are usually mailed within two weeks of an application's receipt. For more information in English or French, call the passport office (tel. 514/283–2152).

Customs and Duties

On Arrival There are two levels of duty-free allowance for travelers entering Great Britain: one for goods bought outside the EC, the other for goods bought in the EC (Belgium, Greece, the Netherlands, Denmark, Italy, Portugal, France, the Irish Republic, Spain, Germany, or Luxembourg).

In the first category, you may import duty-free: 200 cigarettes or 100 cigarillos or 50 cigars or 250 grams of tobacco; two liters of table wine and, in addition, (a) one liter of alcohol over 22% by volume (most spirits), (b) two liters of alcohol under 22% by volume (fortified or sparkling wine), or (c) two more liters of table wine; 50 milliliters of perfume; ¼ liter of toilet water; and other goods up to a value of £36, but not more than 50 liters of beer or 25 cigarette lighters.

In the second category, the EC has set guidelines for the import of certain goods. Following side trips entirely within the EC, you no longer need to go through Customs on your return to the United Kingdom; however, if you exceed the guideline amounts, you may be required to prove that the goods are for your personal use only ("personal use" includes gifts). The guideline levels are: 800 cigarettes, 400 cigarillos, 200 cigars, and 1 kilogram of smoking tobacco, plus 10 liters of spirits, 20 liters of fortified wine, 90 liters of wine, and 110 liters of beer. No animals or pets of any kind can be brought into the United Kingdom without a lengthy quarantine. The penalties are severe and strictly enforced. Similarly, fresh meats, plants and vegetables, controlled drugs, and firearms and ammunition may not be brought into Great Britain.

You will face no customs formalities if you enter Scotland or Wales from any other part of the United Kingdom, though anyone coming from Northern Ireland should expect a security check.

On Departure
U.S. Customs

Provided you've been out of the country for at least 48 hours and haven't already used the exemption, or any part of it, in the past 30 days, you may bring home $400 worth of foreign goods duty-free. So can each member of your family, regardless of age; and your exemptions may be pooled, so one of you can bring in more if another brings in less. A flat 10% duty applies to the next $1,000 of goods; above $1,400, the rate varies with the merchandise. (If the 48-hour or 30-day limits apply, your duty-free allowance drops to $25, which may not be pooled.) Please note that these are the *general* rules, applicable to most countries, including Great Britain.

Travelers 21 or older may bring back one liter of alcohol duty-free, provided the beverage laws of the state through which they reenter the United States allow it. In addition, 100 non-Cuban cigars and 200 cigarettes are allowed, regardless of your age. Antiques and works of art more than 100 years old are duty-free.

Gifts valued at less than $50 may be mailed duty-free to Stateside friends and relatives, with a limit of one package per day per addressee (do not send alcohol or tobacco products, or perfume valued at more than $5). These gifts do not count as part of your exemption, unless you bring them home with you. Mark the package "Unsolicited Gift" and include the nature of the gift and its retail value.

For a copy of "Know Before You Go," a free brochure detailing what you may and may not bring back to the United States, rates of duty, and other pointers, contact the U.S. Customs Service (Box 7407, Washington, DC 20044, tel. 202/927–6724).

Canadian Customs

Once per calendar year, when you've been out of Canada for at least seven days, you may bring in $300 worth of goods duty-free. If you've been away less than seven days but more than 48 hours, the duty-free exemption drops to $100 but can be claimed any number of times (as can a $20 duty-free exemption for absences of 24 hours or more). You cannot combine the yearly and 48-hour exemptions, use the $300 exemption only partially (to save the balance for a later trip), or pool exemptions with family members.

Goods claimed under the $300 exemption may follow you by mail; those claimed under the lesser exemptions must accompany you on your return.

Alcohol and tobacco products may be included in the yearly and 48-hour exemptions but not in the 24-hour exemption. If you meet the age requirements of the province through which you reenter Canada, you may bring in, duty-free, 1.14 liters (40 imperial ounces) of wine or liquor *or* two dozen 12-ounce cans or bottles of beer or ale. If you are 16 or older, you may bring in, duty-free, 200 cigarettes, 50 cigars or cigarillos, and 400 tobacco sticks or 400 grams of manufactured tobacco. Alcohol and tobacco must accompany you on your return.

Gifts may be mailed to friends in Canada duty-free. These do not count as part of your exemption. Each gift may be worth up to $60—label the package "Unsolicited Gift—Value under $60." There are no limits on the number of gifts that may be sent per day or per addressee, but you can't mail alcohol or tobacco.

For more information, including details of duties on items that exceed your duty-free limit, ask the Revenue Canada Customs and Excise Department (Connaught Bldg., MacKenzie Ave., Ottawa, Ont. K1A 0L5, tel. 613/957–0275) for a copy of the free brochure "I Declare/ Je Déclare."

Arriving and Departing

From North America by Plane

Since the air routes between North America and London are heavily traveled, you have many airlines and fares to choose from. But fares change with stunning rapidity, so consult your travel agent on which bargains are currently available.

Flights are either nonstop, direct, or connecting. A **nonstop** flight requires no change of plane and makes no stops. A **direct** flight stops at least once and can involve a change of plane, although the flight number remains the same; if the first leg is late, the second waits. This is not the case with a **connecting** flight, which involves a different plane and a different flight number.

Airlines U.S. airlines serving London include **Delta** (tel. 800/241–4141); **TWA** (tel. 800/892–4141); **USAir** (tel. 800/428–4322); **American Airlines,** which also serves Manchester, England (tel. 800/433–7300); and **Northwest Airlines,** which also serves Glasgow, Scotland (tel. 800/447–4747). U.K. airlines with offices in the United States include **British Airways** (tel 800/247–9297) and **Virgin Atlantic** (tel. 800/862–8621).

From **Downtown to** **the Airports** *To Heathrow* The Piccadilly Line of the Underground connects with Heathrow (all terminals). Trains run every four to eight minutes; journey time is roughly 50 minutes; price is £2.80 one-way. London Transport's *Airbus* service also runs to Heathrow; two routes stop at many central locations, including most major hotels. The A1 leaves every 30 minutes from Victoria Station, daily 6:40 AM–8:15 PM; travel time is about an hour. The A2 leaves Russell Square, near Euston Station, with the same frequency as the A1, daily 6 AM–8:25 PM; travel time is about an hour and 20 minutes. Price for each route is £5 or $10, one-way.

An alternative to the Airbus, serving Heathrow, is the 390 bus, which departs Stand 8, Buckingham Palace Road, weekdays at 7:35, 9:35, 11:05 AM and 1:05, 3:45, 5:20, 6:35, and 9:15 PM (times vary slightly on weekends), stopping at Hyde Park Corner and Kensington High Street. Journey time is about an hour, and the fare is £4 one-way.

By car, the most direct route from central London is via the M4. By taxi, the fare from downtown should be around £25; the journey time will depend on the traffic.

To Gatwick Fast nonstop trains leave Victoria Station every 15 minutes, 5:30 AM–10 PM; five times an hour, 10–midnight; and hourly, midnight–5 AM. Journey time varies from 30 to 39 minutes. Price is £8.69 one-way. Regular bus services are provided by *Green Line Coaches* (tel. 081/668–7261), including the Flightline 777, which leaves Victoria Coach Station hourly, 5:30 AM–11:25 PM. A one-way ticket costs £6. Travel time: about 70 minutes.

By car, take the A23 and then the M23 from central London. Taxis from the city to Gatwick are prohibitively expensive—you may find that it is much more reasonable to take the train.

To Stansted London's third airport opened in March 1991. It serves mainly European destinations, plus American Airlines flights to New York and Chicago and AirTransit flights to Toronto and Vancouver. The terminal is now linked to Liverpool Street via the Stansted Express. Trains run half-hourly and cost £9.80 one-way.

Staying in London

Important Addresses and Numbers

Tourist Information The main **London Tourist Information Centre** at Victoria Station Forecourt (tel. 071/730–3488) provides details about London and the rest of Britain, including general information, tickets for tube and bus, hotel reservations, theater, concert, and tour reservations, and various other services. It's open weekdays and Saturday 8–7, Sunday 8–5. Other information centers are at *Heathrow Airport* (Terminals 1, 2, and 3) and *Gatwick Airport* (International Arrivals Concourse), and, open during store hours only, in *Harrods* (Brompton Rd., SW1 7XL) and *Selfridges* (Oxford St., W1A 2LR).

The **London Travel Service** (Bridge House, Ware, Hertfordshire SG12 9DE, tel. 0920/ 469755) offers travel, hotel, and tour reservations for London (weekdays 9–5:30, Sat. 9–5).

The **British Travel Centre** (12 Regent St., SW1Y 4PQ, tel. 071/730–3400) offers travel, hotel, and entertainment information for the whole of Britain (weekdays 9–6:30, Sat. 10–4).

Embassies and Consulates **U.S. Embassy** (24 Grosvenor Sq., W1A 1AE, tel. 071/499–9000). Located inside the embassy is the American Aid Society, a charity set up to help Americans in distress. Dial the embassy number and ask for extension 570 or 571.

Canadian High Commission (Canada House, Trafalgar Sq., London SW1Y 5BJ, tel. 071/629–9492).

Emergencies For police, fire department, or ambulance, dial 999.

The following hospitals have 24-hour emergency wards: **Guys** (St. Thomas St., SE1, tel. 071/407–7600); **Royal Free** (Pond St., Hampstead, NW3, tel. 071/794–0500); **St. Bartholomew's** (West Smithfield, EC1, tel. 071/600–9000); **St. Thomas's** (Lambeth Palace Rd., SE1, tel. 071/928–9292); **University College** (Gower St., W1, tel. 071/387–9300); **Westminster** (Dean Ryle St., Horseferry Rd., SW1, tel. 071/828–9811).

Pharmacies Chemists (drugstores) with late hours include **Bliss Chemist** (50–56 Willesden La., NW6, tel. 071/624–8000; 5 Marble Arch, W1, tel. 071/723–6116), open daily 9 AM–midnight, and **Boots** (439 Oxford St., W1, tel. 071/409–2857), open Thursday 8:30–7.

Credit Cards Here are the numbers to call for assistance should your credit cards be lost or stolen: **Access (MasterCard)** (tel. 0702/352255); **American Express** (tel. 071/222–9633 for credit cards or 0800/521313 for traveler's checks); **Barclaycard (Visa)** (tel. 0604/230230); **Diners Club** (tel. 0252/516261).

Telephones

Local Calls There are two types of phones, one that accepts coins and one that accepts phone cards.

The coin-operated phones are of the push-button variety; most take all but 1p coins. Insert the coins *before* dialing (minimum charge is 10p). If you hear a repeated single tone after dialing, the line is busy; a continuous tone means the number is unobtainable (or that you have dialed the wrong—or no—prefix). The indicator panel shows you how much money is left; add more whenever you like. If there is no answer, replace the receiver and your money will be returned.

Card phones operate with special cards that you can buy from post offices or newsstands displaying the green and white phone card sign. They are ideal for longer calls, are composed of units of 10p, and come in values of £2, £4, £10, and £20. To use, lift the receiver, insert your card, and dial the number. An indicator panel shows the number of units used. At the end of your call the card will be returned.

For long-distance calls within Britain, dial the area code (which begins with a zero), followed by the number.

In May 1990, London's 01 prefix was replaced by two three-digit prefixes, 071 for inner London, 081 for outer London. You do not need to dial either if calling from inside the same zone, but you will have to dial 081 from an 071 number, and 071 from an 081 number. Drop the zero from the prefix and dial only 71 or 81 when calling London from overseas.

All calls are charged according to the time of day. Peak rate (most expensive) runs weekdays 9 AM–1 PM; standard rate is weekdays 8 AM–9 AM and 1 PM–6 PM; cheap rate is weekdays 6 PM–8 AM and all day on weekends.

International Calls These are usually cheaper when made weekdays between 8 PM and 8 AM, and at any time on weekends. For direct dialing, dial 010, then the country code, area code, and number. For the international operator, credit card, or collect calls, dial 155. For directory inquiries (information) in most countries, dial 153. Bear in mind that hotels usually levy a hefty surcharge on calls made from hotel rooms; it's better to use the pay phones located in most hotel foyers.

Operators and Information To call the operator, dial 100; directory inquiries (information) for London numbers only, 142; information for the rest of Britain, 192. A charge is made for directory inquiries.

Mail

The **London Chief Post Office** (King Edward St., EC1A 1AA, tel. 071/239–5047) is open weekdays 8:30–6. The **Trafalgar Square Post Office** (24–28 William IV St., WC2N 4DL, tel. 071/930–9580) is open Monday–Saturday 8–8. Most other post offices are open weekdays 9–5:30, Saturday 9–12:30 or 1. Stamps may be bought from main or subpost offices (the latter are located in stores), from stamp machines outside post offices, and from many newsagents stores and newsstands. Mailboxes are known as post or letter boxes and are painted bright red; large tubular ones are set on the edge of sidewalks, while smaller boxes are set into post office walls.

Rates Postal rates are: airmail letters up to 10 grams to North America, 39p; postcards 33p, aerogrammes 34p. Letters within Britain are 24p for first class, 18p for second class. Always check rates in advance, however, as they are subject to change.

Receiving Mail If you're uncertain where you'll be staying, you can have mail sent to you c/o Poste Restante, **London Chief Post Office** (King Edward St., EC1A 1AA). The service is free and may be used for three months. You'll need your passport or some other form of identification to claim your mail. Alternatively, **American Express** (6 Haymarket, SW1Y 4BS, tel. 071/930–4411, or any other branch) will accept letters free of charge on behalf of its customers; noncustomers pay 60p per visit to the mailroom.

Getting Around London

By Underground Known colloquially as "the tube," London's extensive Underground system is by far the most widely used form of city transport. Trains run both beneath and above ground out into the suburbs, and all stations are clearly marked with the London Underground circular symbol. (In Britain, the word "subway" means "pedestrian underpass.") Trains are all one class; smoking is *not* allowed on board or in the stations.

There are 10 basic lines—all named—plus the East London line, which runs from Shoreditch and Whitechapel across the Thames and south to New Cross, and the Docklands Light Railway, which runs from Stratford in east London to Greenwich, with an extension to the Royal Docks that should be completed by the time you read this. The Central, District, Northern, Metropolitan, and Piccadilly lines all have branches, so be sure to note which branch is needed for your particular destination. Electronic platform signs tell you the final stop and route of the next train, and some signs also indi-

London Underground

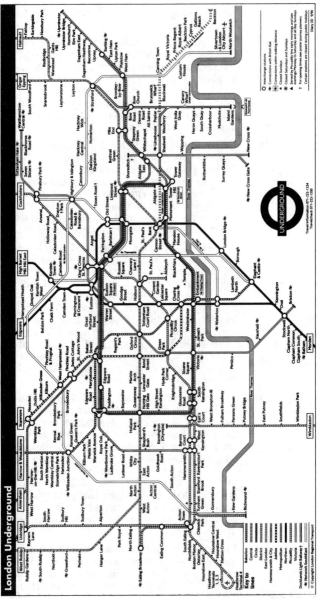

cate how many minutes you'll have to wait for the train to arrive.

Hours From Monday to Saturday, trains begin running just after 5 AM; the last services leave central London between midnight and 12:30 AM. On Sundays, trains start two hours later and finish about an hour earlier. Frequency of trains depends on the route and the time of day, but normally you should not have to wait more than 10 minutes in central areas.

Fares For both buses and tube fares, London is divided into six concentric zones; the fare goes up the farther out you travel. Ask at Underground ticket counters for the London Transport booklet "Tickets," which gives details of all the various ticket options and bargains for the tube; after some experimenting, you'll soon know which ticket best serves your particular needs.

There are LT (London Transport) Travel Information Centres at the following tube stations: Heathrow, daily, varying times at each terminal; Victoria, daily 8:15 AM–9:30 PM; Piccadilly Circus, daily 8:15–6; Oxford Circus, Monday–Saturday 8:15–6; Euston, Monday–Thursday and Saturday 7:15–6, Friday 7:15 AM–7:30 PM, Sunday 8:15–6; and King's Cross, Monday–Thursday 8:15–6, Friday 7:15 AM–7:30 PM, Saturday 7:15–6. For information on all London bus and tube times, fares, etc., call 071/222–1234; the line is operated 24 hours.

By Bus London's bus system consists of bright red double- and single-deckers, plus other buses of various colors. Destinations are displayed on the front and back, with the bus number on the front, back, and side. Not all buses run the full length of their route at all times, so always check the termination point before boarding, preferably with the conductor or driver. Some buses still have a conductor whom you pay after finding a seat, but there are a lot of "one-man" buses on the road, in which you pay the driver upon boarding.

Buses stop only at clearly indicated stops. Main stops—at which the bus *should* stop automatically—have a plain white background with a red LT symbol on it. There are also request stops with red signs, a white symbol, and the word "Request" added; at these you must hail the bus to make it stop. Smoking is not allowed on any bus. Although you can see much of the town from a bus, *don't* take one if you want to get anywhere in a hurry; traffic often slows to a crawl, and during rush hour you may find yourself waiting 40 minutes for a bus and then not being able to get on it once it arrives. If you do go by bus, ask at a Travel Information Centre for a free London Bus Map.

Fares   One-way fares start at 80p in the central zone. Travelcards are good for both tube and bus; there are also bus passes available for daily, weekly, and monthly use, and prices vary according to zones.

By Taxi   Those big, black taxicabs are as much a part of the London streetscape as the red double-decker buses, yet they now come in a variety of colors and some carry advertising on their sides. Hotels and main tourist areas have cab stands (just take the first in line), but you can also flag one down from the roadside. If the yellow "for hire" sign on the top is lit, then the taxi is available.

Fares   Fares start at £1 when the flag falls and increase by units of 20p per 291 yards or 60 seconds. A 40p surcharge is added on weekday nights 8–midnight and Saturday up to 8 PM. The surcharge rises to 60p on Saturday nights, Sundays, and national holidays—except over Christmas and New Year's Eve when it rises to £2. Fares are usually raised in June of each year.

By Car   The best advice about driving in London is: don't. Because the capital grew up as a series of villages, there never was a central plan for London's streets, and the result is a winding mass of chaos, aggravated by a passion for one-way streets.

If you must risk life and limb, however, note that the speed limit is 30 mph in the royal parks, as well as (theoretically) in all streets—unless you see the large 40 mph signs (and small repeater signs attached to lampposts) found only in the suburbs. Other basic rules: Pedestrians have right-of-way on "zebra" crossings (those black-and-white stripes that stretch across the street between two Belisha beacons—orange-flashing globe lights on posts). The curb on each side of the zebra crossing has zigzag markings. It is illegal to park within the zigzag area, or to pass another vehicle at a zebra crossing. On other crossings pedestrians must yield to traffic, but they do have right-of-way over traffic turning left at controlled crossings—if they have the nerve.

Traffic lights sometimes have arrow-style lights directing left or right turns; it is therefore important not to get into the turn lane if you mean to go straight ahead, so try to catch a glimpse of the road markings in time. The use of horns is prohibited between 11:30 PM and 7 AM.

By Boat A high-speed **Riverbus** service, operating catamarans, plies the busiest stretch of the Thames on a regular 15- to 30-minute schedule. The service operates from 7 AM to 8 PM, with more frequent sailings during peak hours. The route covered is from Chelsea Harbour Pier in the west to Greenwich and the City Airport, with stops at Cadogan Pier, Charing Cross, the South Bank Festival Pier, Swan Lane Pier in the City, London Bridge Pier by Hays Galleria, St. Katharine's, Butler's Wharf, Canary Wharf, the Scandic Crown Hotel, and Greenland Piers. The journey time over the complete length of the run is 55 minutes (changing at Charing Cross or Swan Lane), though shorter sections can be as little as five. There is a courtesy bus from Canary Wharf Pier to London City Airport. Fares range from £1.50 to £6. The **Riverbus Explorer pass** costs £6 and gives unlimited travel after 9:30 AM, plus discounts to attractions. Call 071/987–0311 for information.

London Districts Greater London is divided into 32 boroughs—33, counting the City of London, which has all the powers of a London borough. More useful for finding your way around, however, are the subdivisions of London into various postal districts. Throughout the guide we've listed the full postal code for places you're likely to be contacting by mail, although you'll find the first half of the code more important. The first one or two letters give the location: N=north, NW= northwest, etc. Don't expect the numbering to be logical, however. You won't, for example, find W2 next to W3.

Guided Tours

Orientation Tours

By Bus **London Transport's London Plus** guided sightseeing tours (tel. 071/828–6449) offer passengers a good introduction to the city from double-decker buses, which are open-topped in summer. Tours run daily every half-hour, or more during summer, 10–5, from Marble Arch, Victoria, Piccadilly, Harrods, Trafalgar Square, and some 30 more places of interest. You may board or alight at any stop to view the sights, and then get back on the next bus. Tickets (£8 adults, £4 children; £10 or £5 for a two-day pass) may be bought from the driver, in advance from London Transport and Tourist Centres, from London Coaches (Wilton Road, Victoria), or by phone with a credit card (tel. 071/828–6449). Other agencies offering half- and full-day bus tours include **Evan Evans** (tel. 071/930–2377), **Frames Rickards** (tel. 071/837–3111), **Travellers Check-In** (tel. 071/580–8284), and **The Big Bus Company** (tel. 081/944–7810).

By River From April to October, boats cruise the Thames, offering a different view of the London skyline. Most leave from Westminster Pier (tel. 071/930–4097), Charing Cross Pier (Victoria Embankment, tel. 071/839–3312), and Tower Pier (tel. 071/488–0344). Downstream routes go to the Tower of London, Greenwich, and the Thames Barrier; upstream destinations include Kew, Richmond, and Hampton Court. Most of the launches seat between 100 and 250 passengers, have a public address system, and provide a running commentary on passing points of interest. Depending upon destination, river trips may last from one to four hours. For more information, call **Catamaran Cruisers** (tel. 071/839–3572), **Tidal Cruises** (tel. 071/928–9009), or **Westminster Passenger Services Association** (tel. 071/930–4097).

By Canal During summer, narrow boats and barges cruise London's two canals, the Grand Union and Regent's Canal; most vessels (they seat about 60) operate on the latter, which runs between Little Venice in the west (nearest tube:

Warwick Avenue on the Bakerloo Line) and Camden Lock (about 200 yards north of Camden Town tube station). **Jason's Trip** (tel. 071/286–3428) operates one-way and round-trip narrowboat cruises on this route. During April, May, and September, there are two cruises per day; from June to August, there are four. Trips last 1½ hours and cost £3.25 for adults, £2 for children and senior citizens round-trip.

London Waterbus Co. (tel. 071/482–2550) offers the Zoo Waterbus service daily from March to September, on weekends in winter. A round-trip canal cruise, London Zoo–Camden Lock, costs £3.10 adults, £1.80 children. Combined zoo entrance–waterbus tickets are also available.

Canal Cruises (tel. 071/485–4433) also offers cruises from March to October on the *Jenny Wren* (£3.90 adults, £1.80 children and senior citizens), and all year on the floating restaurant *My Fair Lady* (Tues.–Sat. dinner, £24.95; Sun. lunch, £16.95).

Walking Tours One of the best ways to get to know London is on foot, and there are many guided walking tours from which to choose. **The Original London Walks** (tel. 071/624–3978) has a very wide selection and takes justifiable pride in the infectious enthusiasm of its guides. **City Walks** (tel. 071/700–6931), **Streets of London** (tel. 081/346–9255), and **Citisights** (tel. 081/806–4325) are some of the other better-known firms, but you can investigate more tours at the London Tourist Information Centre at Victoria Station. The lengths of walks vary (usually 1–3 hours), and you can generally find one to suit even the most specific of interests—Shakespeare's London, say, or a Jack the Ripper tour. Prices range around £4 for adults.

For those who would rather explore on their own, the City of London Corporation has laid out a **Heritage Walk** leading through Bank, Leadenhall, and Monument streets; follow the trail by the directional stars set into the sidewalks. A map of this walk may be found in *A Visitor's Guide to the City of London*, available from the City Information Centre across from St. Paul's Cathedral. Another option is to follow the **Silver Jubilee Walkway**, created in 1977 in honor of the 25th anniversary of the accession of the present queen. The entire route covers 10 miles and is marked by a series of silver crowns set into the sidewalks; Parliament Square makes a good starting point. Books available from the British Travel Centre (12 Regent St., W1) list other London Regional Transport walks.

Opening and Closing Times

Banks are normally open weekdays 9:30–3:30, but some branches are now open later and provide services on Saturday. Banks at major airports and train stations also have extended hours. **Museums** are usually open Monday–Saturday 10–5 or 10–6, Sunday 2–5 or 2–6, including most national holidays, but not major ones like Christmas Day, Boxing Day (Dec. 26), and New Year's Day. Check individual listings for definite opening hours. **Pubs,** since mid-1988, are generally open Monday–Saturday 11 AM–11 PM, Sunday noon–3 and 7–10 or 10:30, though these hours vary. **Stores** typically stay open Monday–Saturday 9–5:30 or 9–6. Some have late opening hours on Wednesday or Thursday until 7 or 7:30 PM, and in spite of the blue laws, many are open on Sunday.

National Holidays In England and Wales, they're January 1; April 1 (Good Friday); April 4 (Easter Monday); May 2 (May Day Holiday); May 30 (Spring Bank Holiday); August 29 (Summer Bank Holiday); December 25 and 26 (Christmas Day and Boxing Day).

2 Exploring London

Traditionally, London has been divided between the City to the east, where its banking and commercial interests lie, and Westminster to the west, the seat of the royal court and of government. That distinction remains today, as our two most substantial exploring sections—the **City** and **Westminster and Royal London**—demonstrate. The City route has a distinctly financial orientation, while the Westminster exploration roves through history, passing royal palaces, past and present, and surveying the government area around Parliament Square.

London expanded outward from Westminster during the 17th century, the rate of development steadily increasing as the decades passed. Elegant town houses were built for the nobility first in **St. James's** and **Mayfair**, and later in **Chelsea, Knightsbridge,** and **Kensington.** These remain pleasant, if very pricey, residential neighborhoods, as well as being busy, elegant shopping areas, as our walks around them will show.

London also enjoys unique "lungs," a great swathe of greenery across the city center, thanks to its past kings and queens, who reserved large areas for their own hunting and relaxation. The passage of time has inevitably opened them up to the public. The largest of these "royal parks"—no longer monarchical possessions, but administered by a government department—are described in the section on **Hyde Park and Kensington Gardens.**

Westminster and Royal London

Numbers in the margin correspond to points of interest on the Westminster and Royal London map.

The sites covered in this section—Trafalgar Square, Buckingham Palace, the Houses of Parliament, and Westminster Abbey—form what some Londoners know, only slightly facetiously, as the Golden Triangle. You won't find much gold here, but you will find many of London's major tourist attractions within and along the sides of the triangle. All the sights here could easily be seen in a day, though it would be an exhausting one. But you could also devote a month or more to exploring the area and still feel that you were only scratching the surface.

Our description of Westminster takes you from Trafalgar Square to Buckingham Palace, and then to Parliament Square, though there's no reason why you can't go in the opposite, clockwise, direction. Trafalgar Square is the point in London to and from which all distances in the rest of Britain are officially measured, making it the geographical—if not the psychological—center of the capital.

Trafalgar Square and the National Gallery

Trafalgar Square stands on the site of what was originally the Royal Mews, or stables, of the nearby Palace of Whitehall. The square as it is today dates from about 1830, when the central portion was leveled, the National Gallery was begun, and the statue of Lord Nelson, victor of the battle of Trafalgar in 1805, was erected. At the same time, the square's name was changed. **❶ Nelson's Column,** the massive gray column supporting the statue 185 feet up in the air on the summit, is certainly the most famous monument in London, and the dominant landmark in the square. Four huge lions, designed by the Victorian painter Edwin Landseer, guard the base of the column, which in turn is decorated by four massive bronze panels cast from the French guns captured during the Napoleonic wars at the naval battles of St. Vincent, Aboukir Bay, Copenhagen, and Trafalgar itself. Each panel depicts a scene from the battle in which the guns were captured. On either side of Nelson's column is a large fountain. The originals were installed when the square was laid out, but were replaced after World War II. They are the focus of many annual celebrations, particularly New Year's Eve, when great crowds see the new year in. The square has also been the favorite site for political rallies and demonstrations. Less controversial gatherings take place at Christmas, when a huge fir tree is set up in the square. An annual gift from Norway, the tree is that

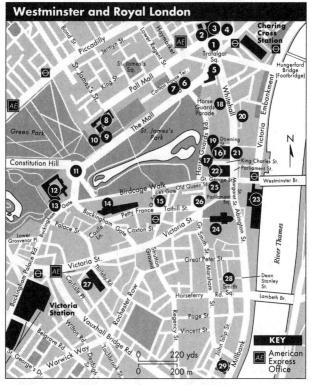

Westminster and Royal London

country's way of saying thank you to the people of Britain for their assistance during World War II.

The north side of Trafalgar Square is formed by the long, low facade of the **National Gallery,** one of the world's great art collections. The Gallery was founded in 1824, and grew rapidly, until by 1900 it had become one of the world's foremost collections. Today, practically every artist of significance from the 15th to the 19th century is represented here.

As you can't see everything in one visit, study the plans prominently displayed as you go in, pick up a free floor plan, and choose those painters or periods that interest you most. Better still, go to the **Micro Gallery,** the computer information center in the Sainsbury Wing, and print out a free personal tour map, highlighting the paintings you most want to see. The Sainsbury Wing, designed by Robert Venturi to house the early Renaissance collection, opened in 1991, following the rehanging of the entire collection. Now more than ever, and in contrast to most other leading London museums, the National Gallery has the advantage of being easy to negotiate. *Trafalgar Sq., tel. 071/839–3321; 071/839–3526 (recorded general information); 071/389–1773 (recorded exhibition information). Admission free; admission charge for special exhibitions. Free 1-hr guided tours start at the Sainsbury Wing weekdays at 11:30 and 2:30, Sat. 2 and 3:30. Open Mon.–Sat. 10–6, Sun. 2–6; June–Aug., also Wed. until 8; closed Good Friday, May Day, Dec. 24–26, Jan 1.*

Outside the Gallery, on the grass slopes in front, stand two small statues. One portrays Charles II's younger brother, James II, who tried unsuccessfully to return Britain to Catholicism. The sculptor was Grinling Gibbons, a brilliant Dutch artist who flourished at the end of the 17th century, and was "Master Carver in Wood to the Crown." At the other end of the facade is George Washington, in a replica of the famous statue by Houdon in Richmond, Virginia, presented to Britain by the Commonwealth of Virginia in 1921.

❸ Just around the corner is the **National Portrait Gallery,** a collection of famous British faces down through the ages. While many of the pictures are not masterpieces, the gallery has a distinctly idiosyncratic and engaging personality, and a uniformity of theme that many other collections lack. The gallery isn't limited to painted portraits; there are busts, photographs, even cartoons. In recent years, the people who work on the displays have shown a real theatrical flair, and many rooms have the effect of stage sets, with drapes, furniture, and other props to set the particular periods. A major expansion has now put much more of the collection on view and added a photography gallery and a separate research center. It helps to visit with a knowledgeable Brit, or pick up explanatory material in the gallery's shop. *2 St. Martin's Pl., tel. 071/ 930–1552. Admission free. Open weekdays 10–5, Sat. 10–6, Sun. 2–6; closed Good Friday, May Day, Dec. 24–26, Jan. 1.*

❹ Just east of the National Gallery is the beautiful church of **St. Martin-in-the-Fields**—not that there are any fields in evidence today. It was built in 1724 and remains among the most distinctive and dignified of London's 18th-century churches, not least for its elegant spire. The church, dedicated to St. Martin of Tours, the patron saint of the poor, still actively carries on its traditional role of caring for the destitute. Its name is also associated with the Academy of St. Martin-in-the-Fields, the well-known orchestra, which was founded here. The church is still used for concerts and recitals, and a candlelit performance here can be a memorable experience. The interior is a bit fusty these days, unlike other churches of the period that have been restored to their original glory. There is a small, semipermanent crafts market in the courtyard behind the church. At the **London Brass-Rubbing Centre** in the crypt of St. Martin's, you can make your own copies from replica tomb brasses (memorial plates), some from churches throughout Britain. Wax, paper, and instructions are provided. *St. Martin-in-the-Fields, Trafalgar Sq., tel. 071/437–6023. Rubbing fee from £1 according to size of brass selected. Open Mon.–*

*Sat. 10–6, Sun. noon–6, closed Good Friday,
Dec. 24–26, Jan. 1.*

Where the southern end of Trafalgar Square
slopes toward Whitehall sits a bronze equestrian statue of Charles I, cast in 1633, on a sadly eroded stone base. It stands on the very
spot where a number of those responsible for
Charles I's execution in 1649—the regicides—
had themselves been executed.

St. James's Park and the Mall

The southwest corner of Trafalgar Square leads
to, and is dominated by, **Admiralty Arch,** so
called because of its proximity to the Admiralty,
headquarters of the Royal Navy. The massive
gray-black arch, with its three great openings,
was built in 1910 to provide a fitting climax to
the Mall (pronounced to rhyme with "shall"),
the great ceremonial way that leads to Buckingham Palace. The central arch is opened only on
ceremonial occasions.

The Mall itself, probably the most splendid and
stately avenue in London, is similarly Edwardian, having been laid out in 1904 to provide a
grand approach to Buckingham Palace. It replaced a more modest street dating from 1660.
Today's avenue lies a little to the south of the
original Mall, which has been preserved as a
wide gravel path. From the Restoration to the
end of the 18th century, the Mall remained by
far the most fashionable spot for London's *beau
monde* to stroll, to see, and to be seen. The tradition survives on Buckingham Palace Garden
Party days in high summer, when the Queen in-
vites hundreds of her subjects, from the grand
and titled to the humble and hardworking, to
don hat and frock and take morning tea with
her—or somewhere near her—on the Buck
House (as Londoners quippingly call the palace)
grounds.

St. James's Park is one of London's smallest
parks, and one of its prettiest. It covers 93 acres
and was developed by a series of monarchs, having originally been the heart of the royal back-
yard when Britain's kings and queens lived in
the sprawling complex of buildings that was
Whitehall Palace. John Nash landscaped it for

George IV, generally giving it the look it has today. Although St. James's Park, with its beautifully maintained flower beds and exotic birds, is a lovely place in which to wander during the day, it is at its best after dark, especially in summer, when the illuminated fountains play and Westminster Abbey and the Houses of Parliament, beyond the trees, are floodlit.

As you walk down the Mall from Trafalgar Square, you will see that much of the right (north) side is occupied by the handsome Regency facade of **Carlton House Terrace,** built by John Nash, an inspired architect and town planner, in 1827–32. Its gleaming white stucco facades and massive Corinthian columns make Carlton House Terrace probably the most imposing and magisterial of all of Nash's many works in London. It stands on the site of Carlton House, built for the Prince Regent in 1709, shortly before the present buildings went up. When George III came to the throne, he decided that splendid though it was, Carlton House was insufficiently magnificent for the king of England, and instructed Nash to rebuild it. Today, Carlton House Terrace is home to a number of institutions and government offices, among them the Royal Society, the Turf Club, and, at ❻ the level of the Mall, the **Institute of Contemporary Arts** (ICA). The ICA offers a varied, often exciting program of theater and performance pieces, exhibitions, films, and lectures. To attend, you have to be a member, but a one-day membership is available. *The Mall, tel. 071/ 930–3647. One-day membership: £1.50 adults, children under 14 free. An additional charge is made for entry to specific events. Open daily noon–11; closed Dec. 24–27, Jan. 1.*

Time Out The **ICAfé** serves delicious hot meals, salads, and quiches, and a good selection of desserts. It's open for lunch and dinner.

Dividing Carlton House Terrace in two are the ❼ magnificent **Duke of York Steps,** named after the statue of George III's second son standing atop a 124-foot column that towers above the steps.

Continuing down the Mall toward Buckingham ❽ Palace, you pass **St. James's Palace** on the right

(*see* St. James's and Mayfair, *below*) and, beyond
it, **Clarence House,** home of the Queen Mother,
and **Lancaster House,** a handsome early 19th-
century mansion used for government receptions and conferences.

Buckingham Palace
to Parliament Square

Buckingham Palace faces the west end of the
Mall and St. James's Park. Planted in the middle
of the great traffic circle in front of the palace is
the **Queen Victoria Memorial,** a huge monument
to the Victorian ideals of motherhood, truth,
justice, peace, and progress. It was put up in
1911 as part of the remodeling of the Mall, and it
makes a wonderful grandstand from which to
view processions and the ceremony of Changing
the Guard. The Guard at Buckingham Palace is
changed daily April through July and on alternate days during the rest of the year. At 11 AM
the Guard marches from Wellington Barracks to
Buckingham Palace: The ceremony itself starts
at 11:30; arrive early if you want a good view.

Buckingham Palace, backed by some 40 acres of
private garden, is the London residence of the
queen. When she is here (usually on weekdays—except in January, some of June, all of
August and September, and when she is away
on state visits), the Royal Standard flies over
the east front. The palace was originally Buckingham House, built in the early 18th century
for the Duke of Buckingham. In 1762 it was sold
to George III. Then, in 1824, Nash was commissioned to remodel the house for George IV, and
its name was changed to Buckingham Palace. It
was then that it became the permanent London
base for the court.

Buckingham Palace is so fixed a symbol of the
crown and of London that few pause to think
how architecturally dull it is, or at least how dull
is the heavy east front added by Sir Aston Webb
in 1913. Initially, the building stood on three
sides of a courtyard, the east end of which was
open to St. James's Park. After Nash remodeled
the rear of the building, which the public never
sees, a new east end was added in 1847, and in
turn reworked by Webb just before World War I.

There are dozens of splendid state rooms inside, including the State Ballroom and, of course, the Throne Room. The royal apartments are in the north wing.

Until very recently the interior was off limits to the public, but a 1992 fire at Windsor Castle created an urgent need for cash. And so Buckingham Palace is now being opened to tourists—on something of an experimental basis through 1997—for eight weeks in August and September, when the royal family is away. *Buckingham Palace Rd., tel. 071/799–2331. Admission: £8 adults, £5.50 senior citizens, £3.50 children under 17. Telephone for hours, which had not been set at press time.*

What was formerly the chapel—bombed during World War II and rebuilt in 1961—is now the **Queen's Gallery,** adjoining the south side of the palace. This is one of the best small galleries in Europe, with regular exhibitions drawn from the vast and spectacular royal collections. *Buckingham Palace Rd., tel. 071/799–2331. Admission: £2 adults, £1 children, £1.50 senior citizens. Open Tues.–Sat. 10–5, Sun. 2–5; closed temporarily between exhibitions. Also closed Mon. (except national holidays), Good Friday, Dec. 24–25, Jan. 1–2.*

About 200 yards from the Queen's Gallery are the **Royal Mews,** where the royal coaches are on view, including the sumptuous State Coach, an immensely elaborate gilded affair, built in 1761. This is the carriage used for coronations. The Royal Mews still serve as stables; thus you should also be able to see some of the horses that draw the coaches in ceremonial processions. *Buckingham Palace Rd., tel. 071/799–2331. Admission: £2 adults, £1 children, £1.50 senior citizens. Combined ticket for Queen's Gallery and Royal Mews: £3.50 adults, £1.50 children, £2.50 senior citizens. Open Wed. noon–4; occasionally closed shortly before state occasions. Also closed during Royal Ascot week in June.*

On the right of the palace as you face it is a wide avenue where the tourist buses park. This is **Constitution Hill,** leading alongside Green Park to Hyde Park Corner. Its name came about when Charles II used to take his daily walk—his constitutional—here. Three attempts on the life of Queen Victoria were made on this road.

In the opposite direction, and from the other side of the Victoria Memorial, **Birdcage Walk** leads along the south side of St. James's Park toward Westminster. The first buildings you pass on the right are the **Wellington Barracks,** the Regimental Headquarters of the Guards Division. These are the elite troops who are traditionally responsible for protecting the sovereign, and who, among many other duties, mount the Guard at Buckingham Palace. **The Guards Chapel** at the far end of the barracks was destroyed by a flying bomb during a service on June 18, 1944, and 121 people were killed. When the dust and rubble settled, it was found that the candles on the altar were still burning. The chapel was rebuilt in the early 1960s, incorporating what was left of the old building. The public is welcome to attend Sunday services, which are held at 11 and 6; the chapel is generally open during the day from about 10 to 3.

The **Guards Museum** occupies an underground set of rooms in the Wellington Barracks. (The entrance to the museum is at the end of the barracks farther from Buckingham Palace, next to the Guard's Chapel.) The museum vividly portrays the story of the five regiments of Foot Guards (Grenadier, Coldstream, Scots, Irish, and Welsh), taking the story from the 1660s right up to the present day. The Royal Case contains the tunic formerly worn by the Queen for the Trooping the Colour. *Wellington Barracks, Birdcage Walk, tel. 071/930–4466, ext. 3430. Admission: £2 adults, 50p children under 16, £1 senior citizens. Open 10–4; closed Fri. and national holidays.*

Off Birdcage Walk, to the right, is a little entry that leads into **Queen Anne's Gate,** lined with 18th-century houses. Tucked away here is a somewhat stiff and formal statue of Queen Anne herself, who reigned from 1702 to 1714 and was the last monarch of the Stuart dynasty. She was popularly known as Brandy Anne, from her favorite tipple, which she disguised in a teapot.

Birdcage Walk runs into Parliament Square, site of Westminster Abbey and the Houses of Parliament. Before reaching it, however, there's an interesting detour to the left off Birdcage Walk. This takes you along **Horse Guards Road,** which runs between Birdcage Walk and the Mall, with St. James's Park on one side and the Foreign Office and Horse Guards Parade on the other.

The magnificently ornate Italianate edifice that **16** is the **Foreign Office** is the dominant building here. It was built in the 1860s by Gilbert Scott, an architect much better known for his fantastical Gothic Revival buildings.

Just beyond the Foreign Office, at the end of King Charles Street, is the entrance to the **17** **Cabinet War Rooms,** a fascinating labyrinth of wartime offices set deep underground to protect them from German bombing. They have been ingeniously restored and provide a glimpse into the working of Britain's wartime High Command. Among the underground maze of rooms are the Cabinet Room, where many of the most important wartime decisions were made, the Prime Minister's Room, where Churchill made many of his celebrated wartime broadcasts, and the Transatlantic Telephone Room, from which Churchill spoke directly to President Roosevelt in the White House. *Clive Steps, King Charles St., tel. 071/930–6961. Admission: £3.60 adults, £1.80 children under 16, £2.70 senior citizens. Open daily 10–5:15; closed Good Friday, May Day, Dec. 24–26, Jan. 1.*

18 Past the Cabinet War Rooms is **Horse Guards Parade,** a substantial square, open toward St. James's Park, with the elegant facade of William Kent's mid-18th-century Horse Guards building forming the bulk of the opposite side. Horse Guards Parade was originally the tilt yard (a place for jousting contests) of Whitehall Palace, with a small guardhouse standing on the site of the present Horse Guards. But the square is most famous as the site every June of the Trooping the Colour, the great military parade that marks the queen's official birthday (her real birthday is in April, but the monarch traditionally has a second, "official" birthday). This is one of the most spectacular events of the

London year, full of pomp and circumstance. The "Colour" (or flag) that is on display belongs to whichever battalion is selected to provide the monarch's escort that year. Until 1986 the queen took the salute on horseback, but nowadays, flanked by members of her family, she takes the salute standing. You can watch the parade up and down the Mall if you get there very early, but it's extremely hard to find a spot from which to view the Trooping itself, and many monarchists prefer to stay home and see it on TV.

Turning back, you soon come to the entrance of **Downing Street,** a pleasant row of 18th-century houses. **Number 10 Downing Street** is the official residence of the Prime Minister, as it has been since it was presented to Sir Robert Walpole in 1732. Eleven Downing Street, the adjoining house, is the official residence of the Chancellor of the Exchequer (the U.K. equivalent of the Secretary of the Treasury). Both buildings were considerably extended in the early '60s, though the facades were untouched. The center of the complex—the hub of the British system of government—is the Cabinet Room on the ground floor of number 10. Unfortunately, Downing Street is railed off, with police in high profile. But you can catch a glimpse of both houses from Horse Guards Road, or, if you walk round to Whitehall, from the other end of Downing Street.

On Whitehall sits the other facade of Horse Guards, where the Queen's Life Guard—cavalry soldiers in magnificent uniforms—stand duty. The Queen's Life Guard changes here at 11 AM from Monday to Saturday, and at 10 AM on Sunday.

Until the end of the 17th century, the entire area between Whitehall and the Thames, from Parliament Square to Trafalgar Square, was taken up by the huge Whitehall Palace, destroyed by fire in 1698. All that remains today is Inigo Jones's **Banqueting House,** halfway down Whitehall on the east side, opposite Horse Guards. The Banqueting House was built in 1625, and it was in front of this building that Charles I was beheaded in 1649. But to today's visitor it's mainly of interest for the magnificent ceiling frescoes in the main hall on the second floor. These were painted by Rubens for Charles I in about 1630; as a reward Rubens received a knighthood and the princely sum of £3,000. *Whitehall, tel. 071/930–4179. Admission: £2.25 adults, £1.50 children under 15, £1.70 senior citizens. Open Mon.–Sat. 10–5; closed Sun., Good Friday, Dec. 24–26, Jan. 1, and at short notice for banquets, so call first.*

Walking toward Parliament Square, you'll come to the **Cenotaph,** a simple white memorial to the dead of both World Wars. It sits in the center of the street, and on Remembrance Day in November the sovereign lays the first tribute of Flanders poppies, symbolic of the blood-red flowers that grew on the death fields of World War II.

The Houses of Parliament

For the final few yards before it enters Parliament Square, Whitehall changes its name to Parliament Street. Entering Parliament Square you are faced with one of the most dramatic views in London. You have passed, on your right, the **Home Office**—built by Gilbert Scott at the same time as the Foreign Office. On the far side of the square is Westminster Abbey, with the little church of St. Margaret's in front of it. The most magnificent sight of all is to the left: the towers, spires, and crenellations of Big Ben, Westminster Hall, and the Houses of Parliament.

Parliament Square itself was laid out by Charles Barry, architect of the Houses of Parliament, in the middle of the 19th century. The square is populated with statues, mainly of prime ministers from the 19th century—Palmerston, Disraeli, and Robert Peel—and Winston Churchill from our own. Opposite these statesmen, outside Westminster Hall itself, are statues of Richard Coeur de Lion (the Lion-Heart) and Oliver Cromwell, while on the far side of the square stands Abraham Lincoln.

The story of the **Houses of Parliament** is intimately bound up with that of Britain's monarchs, as its official name—the **Palace of Westminster**—suggests. In fact, until Henry VIII moved the court to Whitehall Palace in

1512, the Palace of Westminster was the main residence of the monarch. The first palace was built by Edward the Confessor in the 11th century when he moved his court here from the City. This was taken over and expanded by William the Conqueror, Norman conqueror of Britain in 1066, and his son, William Rufus (William II), who built Westminster Hall at the end of the century. **Westminster Hall,** a massively sturdy hall 240 feet long, is the only part of the original building to have survived, though it has been substantially altered over the centuries, not least by Richard II, who added the fine hammer-beam roof in 1397. Thereafter, the Palace of Westminster was successively rebuilt and expanded through the years, becoming, in the process, the meeting place of the Lords and the Commons, the two Houses of Parliament. Originally, Westminster Hall was used as the meeting place for Parliament, but following the Reformation in the 16th century, the deconsecrated St. Stephen's Chapel became the home of the Commons, while the Lords used the White Chamber. This makeshift arrangement continued until 1834, when a great fire swept through the palace, reducing it overnight to a smoking ruin. Apart from Westminster Hall, all that survived was the crypt of St. Stephen's Chapel, since reconsecrated, and the medieval Jewel Tower.

The rebuilding was one of the great triumphs of early Victorian architecture. The project aroused enormous public interest. It was specified that the new building be ". . . in the Gothic or Elizabethan style," chiefly to ensure that it harmonized with neighboring Westminster Abbey and that it reflected the historic roots of Parliament.

The interior is every bit as lavish and splendid as the exterior, though unfortunately not easy for the public to see. Visitors are admitted to the Public Gallery of each House, but usually only after waiting in line for several hours (the line for the Lords is generally much shorter than that for the Commons), or if they have managed to secure tickets through their embassy. The effort is well worth making for anyone with an eye for history and a taste for mid-Victorian art.

The more sumptuously decorated part of the building is the **House of Lords.** This upper chamber is the loose equivalent of the U.S. Senate, though its members are either appointed or take their seats through birth and enjoy considerably less power than American senators. Deep paneling, gorgeous carving and gilding, and rich crimson leather benches set the tone. The **House of Commons,** where the elected members of Parliament meet, is a plainer affair, with much less in the way of decoration, and simple green benches for the members. Some of the most interesting parts of the interior are the public areas, which you will walk through on your way to the Public Galleries, especially those decorated with enormous frescoes, commissioned by Prince Albert, depicting stirring scenes from British history. There are delightful touches throughout, many of them inspired by Pugin, whose thoroughness even extended to designing special Gothic inkwells and umbrella stands, but for security reasons, public tours of the Palace of Westminster are no longer available.

The most famous features of the Houses of Parliament are the towers at each end of the vast complex. At the southern end is the 336-foot-high **Victoria Tower,** reputedly the largest square tower in the world. (At press time it's still shrouded in scaffolding, since it is undergoing a £7.5 million restoration—one of the largest stone-cleaning operations currently underway in Europe—which is scheduled to finish up some time this year.) Whenever Parliament is in session a Union Jack flies from its summit during the day. The tower at the other end is **Big Ben,** or, more properly, St. Stephen's Tower: Big Ben is actually the nickname of the tower's 13-ton bell, on which the hours are struck. It was named for Sir Benjamin Hall, Commissioner of Works when the bell was installed. A light shines from the topmost point of the tower during night sessions of Parliament.

Westminster Abbey

Directly across from the Houses of Parliament is the unmistakable shape of **Westminster Abbey.** The abbey is both the most ancient of London's great churches and the most important. It is here that Britain's kings and queens are crowned, a tradition that dates back to the coronation of William the Conqueror on Christmas Day, 1066. It is here also that many of these same kings and queens are buried.

The first authenticated church on this site was a Benedictine abbey, founded in 970 and dedicated to St. Peter (the official title of the abbey is still the Collegiate Church of St. Peter). But recent historical research indicates that there may have been an earlier church here—possibly even a place of worship to pagan gods long since forgotten.

What *is* certain is that when Edward the Confessor moved his court to Westminster in 1042, he rebuilt the Benedictine abbey, and it was in this new church that William the Conqueror was crowned. Edward's abbey stood for 200 years more until, in 1245, Henry III, determined to make it the largest and most magnificent church in the kingdom, began the slow process of rebuilding it. Much of the east end of Henry's building was complete at his death in 1272, but then work came to a halt for another century. In 1376, Abbot Littlington raised enough money to continue the project, and by about 1420, the abbey was largely complete.

There were two later major additions. The first was the construction of the chapel to the Virgin Mary (at the rear of the building) by Henry VII from 1503 to 1519. Generally known simply as Henry VII's Chapel, this exquisite late-Gothic chapel is probably the finest example of its type in Britain. The second addition came in the mid-18th century when Nicholas Hawksmoor built the twin towers over the west entrance, the main entrance to the abbey. Though a classical architect, Hawksmoor didn't have much difficulty adapting himself to the task at hand, and his towers blend happily with the somber medieval building behind.

The first thing that strikes you as you enter the abbey is the proliferation of monuments, tombs, statues, and tablets. Just inside the great west door is a **memorial to Winston Churchill.** (His burial site is at Bladon in Oxfordshire, just outside Blenheim, where he was born.) Straight ahead, in the center of the nave, is the **Tomb of the Unknown Warrior,** a nameless World War I soldier buried in earth brought with his corpse from France. It is one of the very few floor-level tombs in the abbey over which the countless visitors do not walk. By the tomb hangs a **U.S. Congressional Medal of Honor,** a counterpart to the Victoria Cross awarded by Britain to the Unknown Soldier in Arlington National Cemetery, Washington, DC.

As you wander up the right aisle, you will see memorials to such diverse figures as Robert Baden-Powell, founder of the Boy Scouts; the Wesleys, founders of Methodism; William Congreve, the 18th-century playwright; and Major John André, honored by the British, though a traitor to Americans. Farther on, in the south transept, you come to **Poets' Corner,** filled with memorials to many of Britain's finest writers and composers. Not many of them are actually buried here. The first poet to be entombed here was Geoffrey Chaucer in 1400. The 17th-century poet and playwright Ben Jonson, who lived in the residential part of the Abbey precincts, has the punning epitaph "O rare Ben Jonson," *orare* also being the Latin for "pray for." Shakespeare, Dryden, Samuel Johnson, Sheridan, Browning, and Tennyson are also remembered here. Because of the disreputable lives that poets sometimes lead, a few of Britain's finest poets have not been considered suitable by the Dean for commemorating in a church, so they have had to wait until a Dean of more lenient views was in charge. The plaque to Dylan Thomas arrived in Poets' Corner only at the prompting of American president Jimmy Carter, who visited the Abbey and expressed surprise that his favorite poet had no memorial. There are also two American-born writers commemorated here—Henry James and T. S. Eliot—both of whom became British citizens.

Behind the high altar lie two of the most interesting areas of the abbey: the Chapel of Edward the Confessor and Henry VII's Chapel. This is the area of the royal tombs. Here you'll find a roll call of the royally romantic past, with many of the striking effigies bringing the dead to life:

Edward the Confessor, lying in his own church in the spot to which he was transferred in 1268; Queen Elizabeth I and her sister "Bloody" Mary; Mary, Queen of Scots, magnificently entombed by her son James I; Henry V, his effigy missing the solid silver head that was stolen at the time of the Reformation (it was replaced by a fiberglass copy in 1971); Queen Anne, who had to wear layers of leather petticoats at her coronation here to keep out the abbey's bitter damp; Richard II, his effigy one of the very first carved portraits of an Englishman extant, lying beside his wife, Anne of Bohemia; Edward III, his life of conquest and tumult a contrast to this figure of patriarchal peace. The recent cleaning and repainting of many of the abbey's memorials gives us a wonderful idea of their original splendor.

The focal feature of the **Chapel of Edward the Confessor,** apart from his own massive tomb, is the **Coronation Chair.** This extremely uncomfortable seat was hastily made in about the year 1300 by order of Edward I. The chair encloses the **Stone of Scone** (pronounced "Skoon"), or Stone of Destiny, which has long been a source of friction between England and Scotland. The kings of Scotland were crowned on it—it was used for the coronation of Macbeth's stepson at Scone in 1057. It was carried away from Scotland by Edward I in 1296 but has, over the centuries, become a symbol of Scottish independence. It has been removed from the abbey only three times: once to Westminster Hall for the installation of Oliver Cromwell as Lord Protector, once for safety from German bombers in 1940, and finally by Scottish Nationalists, who stole it one night in 1950 and smuggled it north of the border. (It was discovered and returned six months later.)

Henry VII's Chapel is one of the miracles of Western architecture, and should be savored. It represents the last riot of medieval design in England and is very un-English in its exuberant richness. A pair of binoculars will help you appreciate the small saints and other delightful details too high up to be seen from ground level. The tomb of Henry VII and his wife, Elizabeth of York, is a masterpiece of the Renaissance by

Torrigiano (1472–1528), an Italian artist who is otherwise famous for having broken Michelangelo's nose in a brawl and was banished from Florence because of it. *Broad Sanctuary, tel. 071/222–5152. Admission into nave free, to Poets' Corner and Royal Chapels £3 adults, £1 children under 16, £1.50 students and senior citizens (Royal Chapels free Wed. 6–8 PM). Open Mon., Tues., Thurs., Fri. 9–4, Wed. 9–7:45, Sat. 9–2, 3:45–5, Sun. all day for services only; closed weekdays to visitors during services.*

Outside the west front of the abbey is an archway leading to **Dean's Yard,** a quiet green courtyard, once part of larger gardens. An entry through the buildings that border the yard leads into Little Dean's Yard (private). The area on this side of the abbey was formerly the living quarters for the monks, and now makes up the quarters of **Westminster School,** one of England's prestigious Public Schools. (In England a Public School is an intensely *private* school.) The original school was founded in medieval times to train the abbey clerks.

In the northeast corner of Dean's Yard, immediately to your left as you come in, is the entrance to the **Cloisters.** After the time you have spent absorbing impressions in the abbey itself, a quiet session in the Cloisters is refreshing before emerging into the bustle of London. The Cloisters also contain a good **brass-rubbing center** where you can take impressions from facsimiles of several fine old tomb brasses. *Tel. 071/222–2085. Admission free; fee charged for each brass rubbed, approx. £2.50–£10. Open Mon.–Sat. 9–5:30; Jan.–Feb., phone first to confirm opening; closed Good Friday, Dec. 24–26.*

In the Norman **Undercroft,** off the Cloisters, there is an excellent small museum. Among its treasures are some royal effigies, dressed in their robes, that used to be carried in funeral processions. Since the faces were taken from death masks, they give an impressive idea of how these monarchs, Charles II among them, actually looked. Next door is the **Pyx Chamber,** now restored to its ancient function as the Abbey's treasury. Some fine examples of silver and silvergilt vessels, mainly 16th- and 17th-century pieces, are on display.

Off the Great Cloister is the **Chapter House,** an octagonal structure that was once the center of the abbey's religious life. But it has also been called "the cradle of all free Parliaments," because the King's Council, and later Parliament, met here from 1257 until the reign of Henry VIII. It is one of the great interiors in Europe, not only for its feeling of space, but also for the daring design that was employed, with a single column, like a frozen fountain, sustaining the roof. *Undercroft, Pyx Chamber, and Treasury, tel. 071/222–5152. Joint admission: £1.90 adults, 90p children under 16, £1.40 senior citizens. Open daily 10:30–4; closed Good Friday, Dec. 24–26.*

㉕ Just north of Westminster Abbey, on the edge of Parliament Square, is the ancient church of **St. Margaret's,** where Sir Walter Raleigh lies buried. He was beheaded in nearby Old Palace Yard. William Caxton, the father of English printing, who had two presses nearby, is also buried here. The east window of the church, made in Flanders in 1509, was a gift from Ferdinand and Isabella of Spain. The church is traditionally popular for weddings; Pepys, Milton, and Sir Winston Churchill were all married here. In a niche on the facade of the church is a lead bust of Charles I, looking across the square with a reflective air at the statue of Cromwell, the man who had him executed.

㉖ The large domed building across the road from the west front of Westminster Abbey is **Central Hall,** headquarters of the Methodist Church in Britain. The building, now used mostly for concerts and meetings, was the site of the first General Assembly of the United Nations in 1948. The modern building next to it is the **Queen Elizabeth Conference Centre,** opened in 1986. The largest of its seven conference rooms can accommodate 1,100 delegates.

Westminster Cathedral and the Tate Gallery

There are two detours that can be made from Parliament Square. The first is to Westminster

Cathedral and the second, a little farther afield, is to the Tate Gallery.

For Westminster Cathedral, head south down Victoria Street from the west front of Westminster Abbey. On the right as you walk toward Victoria is **New Scotland Yard,** a far cry from the romantic late-Victorian building on the Thames that Sherlock Holmes knew as Scotland Yard.

㉗ Westminster Cathedral is on the left of Victoria Street, set back about 100 yards from the road. The area in front of the cathedral has been paved and turned into a pleasing piazza.

Westminster Cathedral is the main Roman Catholic church in London and the seat of the Cardinal of Westminster, head of the Roman Catholic Church in Britain. The major part of the building dates from between 1895 and 1903, though it is still partly unfinished inside. It was designed in a richly Byzantine idiom, as foreign a style as can be imagined in the heart of London. A choral service, especially on a great religious occasion, with the choir singing from its place behind the main altar, provides a memorable experience.

Unfinished as it is, the interior is a slightly mysterious and shadowy amalgam of brick, marble, and mosaic. The marbles come from all over the world—Greece, Italy, Ireland, even Norway. The nave of the cathedral, the widest in the country, is topped by three shallow domes of blackened brick. It is unlikely that the building will ever be finished. The **campanile** (bell tower), on the north side of the church, can also be visited; an elevator will take you up to the top. *Ashley Pl., tel. 071/834-7452. Admission to tower: £2 adults, 50p children, £1 senior citizens. Cathedral open daily, tower open Apr.–Sept.*

To get to the Tate Gallery from Westminster Cathedral, head down Abingdon Street past the front of the Victoria Tower and take the first right down Great College Street. Here, take the first left, down Barton Street. Between Barton Street and Smith Square, the principal destination of this mini-walk, are a series of delightful little early 18th-century town houses. Today, many of them have been bought by Members of Parliament (MPs) and others with business at Westminster. From Barton Street continue down to the end of the road—about 50 yards or so—turn left and then right and head straight down Lord North Street. Ahead of you is Smith

㉘ Square and the Baroque **church of St. John,** or at least what used to be a church. Today, it has been deconsecrated and is used for concerts, and a more delightful concert hall would be hard to find. The church was originally built around 1710. From Smith Square head left up Dean Stanley Street. This brings you out to Millbank, and back to the main route to the Tate Gallery.

Time Out The crypt of St. John's houses a very attractive cafeteria, the **Footstool.** It is open for lunch weekdays and on concert evenings from 5:30.

㉙ The **Tate Gallery** was opened in 1897, and has been extended four times as its holdings have grown. The paintings divide into two main groups: the British collection, an unrivaled series of British paintings from Elizabethan times to the present, and the modern collection, a comprehensive assemblage of modern European and American works. The Tate's director, Nicholas Serota, has revolutionized the way the vast collection is displayed. Early in 1990 he introduced a new policy whereby the collection is completely rehung every nine months, with a heavier emphasis on British works than previously, when they had been relegated to the sidelines in favor of leading non-British artists. The only problem of the exciting new scheme is that a visitor cannot rely on seeing an old favorite, as it might be in storage for a long period.

Don't miss the Turner collection, housed in the **Clore Gallery,** opened in 1987. J.M.W. Turner (1775–1851) bequeathed the works that remained in his studio at his death to the nation with the stipulation that they should be displayed in one place. The Clore Gallery, whose design (by Sir James Stirling, who died in 1992) caused a lot of controversy, shows these works in rotation. *Millbank, tel. 071/821–1313 or 071/ 821–7128 (recorded information). Admission free; admission charged for special exhibitions.*

*Open Mon.–Sat. 10–5:50, Sun. 2–5:50; closed
Good Friday, May Day, Dec. 24–26, Jan. 1.*

Time Out The cafeteria in the Tate Gallery basement is a
pleasant place to relax after the exertions of picture gazing; it has a good selection of cakes,
sandwiches, and light lunches.

St. James's and Mayfair

*Numbers in the margin correspond to points of
interest on the St. James's and Mayfair map.*

The areas covered in this section make up the
heart of the West End, which is the real center
of town, even for Londoners. Nowadays other
neighborhoods may rival these for sophistica-
tion, but here are the biggest hotels, the best
restaurants (or some of them), the most expensive and glamorous shops (alongside some of the
tackiest), and the most snobbish office addresses. It's all very urban and cosmopolitan,
but—Leicester Square and Soho excepted—the
area still tends to empty like a ghost town after
midnight.

As with so much of the center of London, there's
no single obvious route into or around any of the
sections covered here. Look at any map and
you'll quickly see what a random pattern these
streets make. The easiest approach is the
serendipitous one—follow your instincts and
see where they take you.

St. James's

St. James's has a street plan that has barely
changed since it was laid out in the late 17th century. Bounded by Green Park to the west, Haymarket to the east, Piccadilly to the north, and
the Mall to the south, St. James's is the ultimate
enclave of the old-fashioned gentleman's London. This is where you'll find the capital's most
celebrated and distinguished men's clubs and
shirt, shoe, and hat shops (though not tailors—
they're just a step north in Mayfair's Savile
Row). Likewise, the area is liberally sprinkled
with discreet art galleries. St. James's, in

short, exudes an air of dusty elegance and old-fashioned charm.

① Begin your tour of St. James's from **Trafalgar Square,** though you could just as easily begin from Piccadilly or the Mall. From Trafalgar Square, take Cockspur Street or Pall Mall East, on either side of Canada House, to the foot of **②** **Haymarket,** so named because of the horse fodder sold here until 1830. This is a wide and busy thoroughfare, sloping up to Piccadilly Circus at its northern end. It boasts two theaters—the Theatre Royal, built in 1820, and Her Majesty's—plus the Design Centre (which shows examples of the best of modern British design), a clutch of movie theaters, the American Express offices, and New Zealand House, a high-rise at the end of the street. Behind this **③** last building is Nash's **Royal Opera Arcade,** home of some very English little shops selling fishing tackle, old prints, cashmere, and books.

Heading east along Pall Mall for 100 yards or so, past the stately cream facade of the Institute of Directors on your left, you come to the elongated square that is **Waterloo Place.** The column **④** to your left is the **Duke of York memorial** at the head of the **Duke of York Steps,** and around it stands a cluster of statues.

Diagonally opposite this collection of frozen worthies is the glistening facade of the **⑤** **Athenaeum,** founded in 1824 for the intellectual elite of London. Artists, writers (including J. M. Barrie, Arthur Conan Doyle, Rudyard Kipling, and Joseph Conrad), scientists, and top churchmen and politicians were members, but—as in all the institutions of London's "Clubland"—women were personae non gratae. They still are. In fact, none of these exclusive haunts is open to any section of the general public, and membership is nearly impossible to come by. But almost all of the clubs are housed in handsome, sturdy buildings, and you can sometimes peek through the windows. Around the corner from the Athenaeum is the **Travellers'** **⑥** Club and, next door, the **Reform Club,** perhaps the most famous of all and certainly the most attractive, housed in a sooty and stately Italianate

St. James's and Mayfair

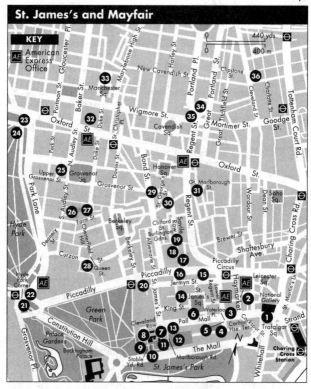

building designed by Charles Barry, architect of the Houses of Parliament.

From the Athenaeum, Pall Mall (pronounced "Pal Mal"), a dignified, elegant road, runs west to St. James's Palace. Its name, like that of the parallel Mall, comes from the early form of croquet—*pail mail* or *pell mell*—that was played here from the beginning of the 17th century to the Restoration. Heading down Pall Mall, you pass, on your left, the **RAC Club**, another of the great St. James's clubs, and, a little beyond it, a series of handsome 17th-century facades. Thomas Gainsborough, the 18th-century painter, lived at #80–82.

❼ Pall Mall ends at **St. James's Palace.** For a century or more this lovely brick palace has taken a back seat in the affairs of the nation, until being co-opted by the Prince of Wales, following his marriage troubles, as his London residence. Its other remaining claims to fame are that a number of royal functionaries have offices here, and that various court functions are held in the State Rooms. However, all foreign ambassadors to Britain are still officially accredited to the "Court of St. James's." The palace originally took its name from the leper hospital that stood here in the 11th century. In the 1530s, Henry VIII knocked the old palace down and began work on the present building. Although it remained a royal residence, it was overshadowed by the sprawling mass of nearby Whitehall Palace. St. James's partly regained royal favor when Whitehall burned down in 1698, despite the preference of the reigning monarchs—William and Mary—for Kensington Palace and Hampton Court. But Queen Victoria finally downgraded St. James's when she came to the throne in 1837 and moved into Buckingham Palace. If St. James's Palace no longer has a prominent role to play, it nonetheless remains the most romantic of London's palaces, especially the facade fronting Pall Mall, made all the more picturesque by the guardsmen standing sentinel outside.

Inside the palace is the **Chapel Royal,** said to have been designed for Henry VIII by Holbein, though heavily redecorated in the mid-19th century. The ceiling still has the initials *H* and *A*, intertwined, standing for Henry VIII and his second wife, Anne Boleyn, the mother of Elizabeth I and the first of Henry's wives to lose her head. *It is possible to attend the Sun. morning services here at 8:30 and 11:15 between the 1st week of Oct. and Good Friday.*

⑧ If you continue along Cleveland Row (the extension of Pall Mall), **York House**—the home of the duke and duchess of Kent —is on the left. A left turn into Stable Yard Road will bring you to **⑨** **Lancaster House.** This was originally built for the Duke of York in the 1820s and was then enlarged in 1833–41. Today it is used by the government for official receptions and conferences. It has been open to the public in the past, but for the moment it remains closed.

⑩ On the other side of Stable Yard is **Clarence House,** so called because it was designed by Nash and built in 1825 for the future king, William IV, then the Duke of Clarence. It was restored in 1949, and is now the London home of the Queen Mother.

Walk back along the Mall toward Admiralty Arch past the south side of St. James's Palace. This Mall frontage was designed by Wren in the 17th century and contrasts well with the Tudor frontage on Pall Mall. To continue your exploration of this little enclave of royal houses, turn back up Marlborough Road, toward Pall Mall **⑪** again. On the left is the open-sided **Friary Court** **⑫** of St. James's Palace, opposite **Marlborough House,** the latter built by Wren for the Duke of Marlborough in 1709 and now the Commonwealth Conference Centre; the building may be open again in 1993 after renovations.

⑬ Just in front of Marlborough House is the **Queen's Chapel,** built for Henrietta Maria, the Roman Catholic wife of Charles I. The chapel is one of London's forgotten glories—small but exquisite. It was built by Inigo Jones between 1623 and 1627 and is one of the first purely classical buildings in the country. *You can attend Sun. services here Easter–July; Holy Communion is celebrated at 8:30 AM and either Sung Eucharist or Morning Prayer at 11:15.*

St. James's continues north from here, up the hill to Piccadilly, by way of **St. James's Street,** which features several more exclusive clubs, including White's, at #37–38, the oldest London club (founded in 1736); Boodle's, #28; Brooks, on the corner of Park Place; and the Carlton, #69. Lobb's, at #9, is a world-famous bespoke shoemaker *(custom* shoemaker), and James Lock, at #6, has been making hats for more than 200 years. The window of this classic shop is always a slightly dusty delight. In contrast to these old-fashioned glories is a startlingly modern copper-colored building halfway up St. James's Street on the left, looking like a group of organ pipes posing as space rockets.

There are two good ways into the heart of St. James's from here: one down King Street, the other down Jermyn Street. Both run right (eastward) off St. James's Street. **King Street** will take you past the solemn 18th-century facade of Christie's, the fine-art auctioneers. The building is open to anyone who cares to step inside and wander around the sale rooms. There's nearly always something of interest about to come under the hammer, including, from time to time, works that will fetch millions. Past Christie's, you come to Duke Street on your left, home to a series of exclusive little galleries; farther on lies **St. James's Square,** one of the oldest and most pleasing of London's elegant leafy squares. The cramped building in its northwest corner is the **London Library,** the most exclusive and probably the best private lending library in London, with about a million volumes lining its creaking shelves.

Take the center exit on the north side of St. James's Square up to **Jermyn Street** and you'll find yourself surrounded by London's best tie- and shirtmakers, as well as stores selling traditional ivory-backed hairbrushes, silk robes, cashmere sweaters, beautiful handmade shoes, and a host of other essential gentlemen's accessories. From Jermyn Street it is no more than a couple of minutes' walk up to Piccadilly, the next stop on our tour.

Piccadilly

Piccadilly Circus, once the hub of the West End and a symbol of London worldwide, makes a convenient starting point for the walk down Piccadilly itself or for a foray northwest into the center of elegant Mayfair. (Of course, *circus* here means a circular street junction; *Piccadilly* is the name of both the district and its principal street.) For our purposes, we treat Piccadilly as separate from Mayfair, but, walking its length, you can head north into Mayfair at any point up any one of the dozen or so streets off Piccadilly.

Piccadilly Circus is rapidly losing its old reputation as London's version of Times Square. Seemingly endless restoration of the surrounding buildings, constant changes of the traffic patterns, and a generally upbeat attitude on the part of local government have all helped to improve the area's grimy image. The most famous inhabitant of the Circus, Eros, has been cleaned, repaired, and relocated. The statue is not actually of Eros at all, but is rather an allegory of Christian Charity, a reference to the original building of Piccadilly Circus and Shaftesbury Avenue in the last century under the patronage of Lord Shaftesbury, a notable philanthropist, who swept away some of the capital's worst slums. The name *Piccadilly* is said by some (although there are several theories) to be derived from the tailor's shop that stood there in the 17th century, and which sold lace collars or "piccadells."

Piccadilly Circus lies at the junction of four major roads: Piccadilly, Regent Street, Shaftesbury Avenue, and Lower Regent Street. Of these, **Piccadilly** is the largest and most prominent. From the Circus it runs due west down to Hyde Park Corner. Care is needed when crossing it as buses go westward against the eastward flow of the rest of the traffic. It is lined by a mixture of stores, airline offices, learned societies, and large hotels—including one of London's most famous, the Ritz.

Walking from Piccadilly Circus, the first building to notice, on the left, is **St. James's Church,** one of Wren's churches, revealing his hand in every elegant line. It was built between 1676 and

1684, but was damaged during the Blitz and
since restored. The spire was not replaced until
1968 and, believe it or not, is made of fiberglass.
There is a wealth of beautiful craftsmanship inside, including a limewood reredos (an ornamental screen behind the altar) by Grinling Gibbons,
who also carved the organ case and the font. The
church is surrounded by a paved garden where
you can rest in the middle of a busy day. A crafts
market is held here on weekends. The church
also offers a lively program of talks, discussions,
and recitals, held on both weekdays and weekends.

Time Out **The Wren at St James's** is a pleasant little café attached to St. James's Church. Sandwiches and
pastries are always on sale, and at lunch or
weekday dinner you can buy salads, soup, and a
hot dish.

Continuing along Piccadilly, you'll pass some famous shops, including **Hatchard's**, one of the
16 best bookshops in London, and **Fortnum and
Mason**, the Queen's grocer. Fortnum's has three
tea shops of varying degrees of elegance (and
price) for mid-sightseeing snacks. Here, too,
is **Piccadilly Arcade**, with tall, glass-fronted
shops.

On the north side of Piccadilly is the Italianate
17 bulk of **Burlington House**, home of the **Royal
Academy of Arts**. The Academy (otherwise
known as the RA) mounts prestigious loan exhibitions, as well as the famous—or infamous, depending on your artistic point of view—Summer
Exhibition of mixed amateur and professional
works. A glass staircase leads up to the entrance
to the Sackler Galleries—a cool white space, designed by Norman Foster, that opened in 1991.
There are some fine works in the permanent collection, but the prize is a bas-relief sculpted
disk, or tondo, by Michelangelo: the *Madonna
Taddei.* Around the courtyard of Burlington
House are several other societies: the Geological
Society, the Chemistry Society, the Linnean
Society, the Society of Antiquaries, and the
Royal Astronomical Society. In short, Burlington House represents nothing less than a little
corner of 18th-century inquiry and investiga-

tion in the middle of London. *Burlington House, Piccadilly, tel. 071/439–7438 or 071/439–4996 (recorded information). Admission varies according to exhibition. Open daily 10–6; closed Good Friday, Dec. 24–26, Jan. 1.*

Time Out   The Royal Academy's restaurant is a pleasant place to have mid-morning coffee, afternoon tea, or a light lunch. You can use it without having to buy an entrance ticket to the current exhibition.

⑱ Running up beside Burlington House is **Burlington Arcade,** a long, covered walkway of delightful little shops. This is the place to wander on a wet day, or to search for an extravagant present to take home. Most of the shops stock traditional British-crafted goods with an emphasis on woolens, linen, glass, and china. It was the first shopping precinct of its kind in the country, and was built for Lord Cavendish in 1819. The Regency atmosphere has been retained right down to the uniformed watchmen (beadles).

⑲ If you turn right at the top of the Burlington Arcade, you will find the **Museum of Mankind,** the British Museum's Department of Ethnography, housed at the back of Burlington House. The department will eventually vacate Burlington House for its move back to the museum proper, but for the time being it remains in its uncrowded, elegant home by the commercial art galleries of Cork Street. It contains a large part of the British Museum's collection of Aztec, Mayan, African, and other ethnic artifacts, all imaginatively displayed. Phone for details of the current exhibition. *6 Burlington Gdns., tel. 071/437–2224. Admission free. Open Mon.–Sat. 10–5, Sun. 2:30–6; closed Good Friday, May Day, Dec. 23–26, Jan. 1.*

Along Piccadilly there are more shops and airline offices, including that of Aeroflot, with a coolly conceived modern equestrian statue by Elizabeth Frink outside. A few blocks ahead the
⑳ **Ritz** hotel looms on the left.

Here, on the south side of Piccadilly, is the northern edge of **Green Park,** a 53-acre expanse of grass and trees. On weekends its railings facing Piccadilly are festooned with art and ornamental objects of all kinds for sale, lending a little color (but not a lot of class) to an otherwise staid stretch.

At the western end of Piccadilly you come to **Hyde Park Corner,** a perpetual maelstrom of traffic at the junction of several major roads. The center of this traffic whirl, however, is an island of surprising tranquillity. There are a few fine statues here, but the centerpiece is the **Wellington Arch,** a triumphal arch that was originally intended as a sort of monumental back gate to Buckingham Palace. London's smallest police station is located in the arch. In order to cross the roadways here, you'll have to use the network of pedestrian underpasses. Each entry is numbered and there are maps on the walls to tell you where to go.

On the north side of Hyde Park Corner, just by the park itself, is **Apsley House,** now the **Wellington Museum.** It was built in the 1770s by Robert Adam, though refaced and extended in the 1820s, by which point it had passed into the hands of the duke, who kept it as his London house until his death in 1852. In 1947, when it was acquired by the nation, it became the Wellington Museum. The interior is much as it was in the Iron Duke's day, full of heavy and ornate pieces, some perhaps more impressive than beautiful, though there's also a fine equestrian portrait of Wellington by Goya, painted during the Peninsula Campaign. Unfortunately, the museum is closed until at least June 1994. *149 Piccadilly, tel. 071/499–5676. Phone for reopening date and new admission prices.*

Mayfair

Mayfair represents all that is gracious in London living, with an unmistakable air of wealthy leisure even on the busiest days. Like neighboring Soho, it is one of the few areas of London whose borders are quite distinct. And, again like Soho, it is laid out on the next best thing to a grid pattern London can offer. This makes it easier to explore. Mayfair is bounded by Piccadilly on the south, Park Lane on the west, Oxford Street on the north, and Regent Street on the east. From all these main roads many streets lead you into this desirable heart of mon-eyed London.

For simplicity's sake, begin your exploration of Mayfair at Hyde Park Corner. Head north from here up Park Lane, the western border of May-fair. **Park Lane,** with its expansive views over Hyde Park, was once one of the most distin-guished Mayfair addresses. But its town houses have mostly been demolished, replaced by a looming series of hotels and office blocks. Yet two groups of the original early 19th-century houses remain overlooking the park, all with de-lightful bow fronts and wrought-iron balconies.

㉓ Continue up Park Lane to **Marble Arch** at the meeting point of Oxford Street and Bayswater Road, another traffic whirlpool. The arch was brought here from Buckingham Palace in 1851, and was sited near the place where the public gallows known as Tyburn Tree once stood. To the west of Marble Arch, at the northeastern **㉔** corner of Hyde Park, is **Speakers' Corner,** a large open space where anyone with the compulsion to air his or her views in public can do so on Sunday afternoons. As the preserve of every kind of ec-centric, this is one of the best free shows in Lon-don. From Marble Arch you can either head down Oxford Street (*see below*) or, to penetrate the heart of Mayfair, backtrack four blocks down the east side of Park Lane to Upper Brook **㉕** Street. This will bring you to **Grosvenor** (pro-nounced "Grove–nor") **Square** and the **U.S. Em-bassy.** This large, graceful square was laid out in 1725–31, and has at its center a statue of Frank-lin D. Roosevelt, erected in 1948. The British public had a soft spot for Roosevelt, which they demonstrated by the speedy way they raised money for the statue. The embassy takes up the whole of one side of the square. John Adams, first American ambassador to Britain and sec-ond president of the United States, lived nearby at the corner of Brook and Duke streets.

From Grosvenor Square walk down South Audley Street. Just over Mount Street is the **㉖** charming little **Grosvenor Chapel**, built in 1730 and used by American servicemen during World

War II. To the left of the church is an entrance to **St. George's Gardens,** a peaceful spot with a fountain in the middle. If you cross the gardens (27) to Farm Street you will find the Jesuit **Church of the Immaculate Conception,** built in the mid-19th century and noted today for its fine music. Chesterfield Hill and then Queen Street will take you down to **Curzon Street,** which crosses Mayfair from west to east. This street retains some old houses amid the modern office blocks. On its south side is an area of considerable charm—**Shepherd Market,** a network of narrow (28) streets with attractive houses and shops. You won't find any sheep there nowadays, though something of a village atmosphere remains, but there are a couple of rousing pubs, and a few anonymous-looking houses that are vestiges of Shepherd Market's red light days.

At the end of Curzon Street, Fitzmaurice Place curves into **Berkeley** (pronounced "Barkly") **Square.** It was once one of London's most distinguished residential squares, and former inhabitants include the prime minister Robert Walpole (1676–1745) and Robert Clive ("Clive of India"; 1725–74).

The heart of modern Mayfair is **Bond Street** (from Berkeley Square, walk along Bruton Street). It is divided into Old and New Bond Street. (Old Bond Street was laid out some 20 years before New Bond Street, in 1690 to be exact.) The older street hasn't lost its air of slight superiority, and today it is the home of many of London's most luxurious shops. Internationally known names like Asprey's and Cartier's are here, as well as some of the top art dealers, and (29) the great auction house of **Sotheby's.** This is a shopping street par excellence.

Near the top of Bond Street, Brook Street leads east to **Hanover Square.** Turn south down St. George's Street and you'll pass the lovely church (30) of **St. George's,** still a top choice for society weddings. Farther down, Clifford Street will take you through to **Savile Row,** renowned for fashionable tailoring since the mid-19th century—though proposed increases in property taxes threaten to force the tailors out into suburbia.

We can wire money to every major city in Europe almost as fast as you can say, "Zut alors! J'ai perdu mes valises".

How fast? We can send money in 10 minutes or less, to 13,500 locations in over 68 countries worldwide. That's faster than any other international money transfer service. And when you're *sans* luggage, every minute counts.

MoneyGram from American Express® is available throughout Europe. For more information please contact your local American Express Travel Service Office or call: 44-71-839-7541 in England; 33-1-47777000 in France; or 49-69-21050 in Germany. In the United States call 1-800-MONEYGRAM.

MoneyGram℠

INTERNATIONAL MONEY TRANSFERS.

519 M.P.H.

190 M.P.H.

75 M.P.H.

0 M.P.H.

WE LET YOU SEE EUROPE AT YOUR OWN PACE.

Regardless of your personal speed limits, Rail Europe offers everything to get you over, around and through anywhere you want in Europe. For more information, call your travel agent or **1-800-4-EURAIL.**

OFFICIAL DISTRIBUTOR
Rail Europe
OF THE EURAIL PASS

Regent and Oxford Streets

The eastern border of Mayfair is **Regent Street,**
which has some good shops, of which the best is
③ **Liberty,** a store filled with rich silks and high
fashion. The Regent Street frontage is surmounted by impressive carvings and a 115-foot
frieze celebrating trade with exotic places.
Around the corner in Great Marlborough
Street, its mock Tudor facade masks a rich interior partly built from the carved timbers of old
warships.

At its northern end, Regent Street meets Oxford Street at **Oxford Circus,** one of the major
traffic junctions in the West End. **Oxford Street**
itself extends west from Oxford Circus to Marble Arch and east to Tottenham Court Road. For
most of its length it is closed to all traffic other
than buses and taxis, though this does not affect
the enormous crowds of people that throng up
and down it. Oxford Street claims to be the capital's premier shopping street, but, despite the
presence of some good department stores, the
majority of the shops here are unmemorable and
offer cheap fashions at high prices. Three stores
③ worth fighting the crowds for are **Selfridges,**
founded by an American businessman; two
branches of that English institution **Marks and
Spencer;** and **John Lewis.** To avoid the worst of
the crowds, try to do your browsing first thing in
the morning.

There are two interesting detours to be made
north from Oxford Street. The first is to the
③ **Wallace Collection,** one of the most delightful
and unexpected art galleries in London. To
reach it, head north from Oxford Street up Duke
Street, beside Selfridges, into Manchester
Square, a typical mid-18th-century London
square with a garden in the center and fine town
houses all around. On the northern side is the
handsome Hertford House, home of the Wallace
Collection.

Because it was first and foremost a private
house, the Wallace Collection has none of that
intimidating formality that so many grand picture galleries possess. Not unlike the Frick Collection in New York, the works here blend
happily with their sumptuous surroundings,

making the entire place a pleasure to walk around. At the heart of the collection are the 18th-century French works—all snapped up at bargain prices by the second marquess during the French Revolution. Boucher, Watteau, Fragonard, and Chardin are all well represented, forming a collection of greater value than its counterpart in the National Gallery. But there are also a number of very fine Rubenses and Rembrandts, Frans Hals's *Laughing Cavalier*, an exquisite Poussin, some stirring Van Dycks, an extensive series of Canalettos, and a whole host of lesser Dutch works from the 17th and 18th centuries. There are also various rooms of fine porcelain and china, arms and armor, and magnificent furniture. As if this were not enough, the collection is almost always uncrowded. *Hertford House, Manchester Sq., tel. 071/935-0687. Admission free. Open Mon.–Sat. 10–5, Sun. 2–5; closed Good Friday, May Day, Dec. 24–26, Jan. 1.*

The other side trip from Oxford Street is up Regent Street north of Oxford Circus to **Portland Place,** of interest to any student of architecture. Heading up Regent Street you see the distinctive circular portico and spire of **All Souls, Langham Place** about 400 yards in front of you.

The **Langham Hotel,** opposite All Souls, was built in 1864 to resemble a Florentine palace and duly played host to exiled royalty (Haile Selassie of Ethiopia, Napoleon III of France) and the *beau monde* of the next 85 years until falling afoul of fashion (new luxury hotels were built farther west) and then, in 1940, a German land mine. Now it has been restored and reopened by the Hilton group.

Directly to one side of All Souls is **Broadcasting House,** headquarters of the British Broadcasting Corporation (BBC). Here, Regent Street becomes Portland Place, one of London's most elegant thoroughfares. It was designed by the brothers Adam in the 1780s, and, when built, was London's widest street. Many of its houses are today in varying states of disrepair, while some have been replaced by slablike prewar blocks.

Clipstone Street (which runs off Great Portland Street) will provide you with a startling view of a modern building of a very different sort—the Post Office Tower, now officially the **British Telecom Tower.** A pencil-thin glass tube built in 1965 and some 620 feet high, it is London's principal telecommunications center. It can be seen from all over London, peeping out from behind even the tallest buildings. However, the best complete top-to-bottom view is from Clipstone Street. The viewing platform at the top was closed to the public some years ago after a bomb scare.

The northern end of Portland Place gives way to Nash's beautiful Park Crescent, the Marylebone Road, and Regent's Park.

Knightsbridge and Kensington

Numbers in the margin correspond to points of interest on the Knightsbridge and Kensington map.

This route takes the London explorer through two fashionable quarters. High society, with its snazzy shops and eating places, is the keynote, although there are also some historic sites to explore. This is an ideal route for a sunny spring or fall day, when London is at its best.

Knightsbridge

Take the Underground to Knightsbridge station and come out the Sloane Street exit. Don't let the chaotic traffic send you back below! One way leads south down Sloane Street to Sloane Square and Chelsea, with the Cadogan Hotel halfway down—where Oscar Wilde foolishly allowed himself to be arrested. Another way, **Knightsbridge,** leads along the south side of Hyde Park and the high-rise that is the Hyde Park Barracks. You might look up and see horses on what appears to be a balcony, for this is the headquarters of the Household Cavalry—perhaps the most glamorous regiment in the British Army, whose gorgeous plumed helmets, sparkling breastplates, and proud, high-stepping horses are always so striking a feature of London's royal occasions. The soldiers regularly exercise their horses in the park, usually first thing in the morning.

Brompton Road, on the left as you leave the station, runs down to Harrods and then on to the great museum complex of South Kensington. ❶ This is an area of ritzy shops, with **Harrods** leading the bunch. Most visitors will buy something here, however small, just to get one of the famous green-and-gold bags. One of the main points of interest is the ground-floor **Food Hall,** with its fine tiled ceiling and decorative array of edibles. But as a modern luxury store Harrods doesn't really compare with some of the best in the United States. It is also desperately crowded, especially at sale time. Try to get there at 10 when it opens.

Time Out **Patisserie Valerie** (215 Brompton Rd., tel. 071/832–9971; open daily), just down the road from Harrods, offers light meals and a heartbreakingly beautiful array of pastries. It's a perfect spot for breakfast, lunch, or tea.

There are a few other highlights along Brompton Road, especially Beauchamp (pronounced "Beecham") Place, with dress and shoe boutiques for the well-lined purse, and a generous sprinkling of restaurants and wine bars. Walton Street, running off Beauchamp Place, is also a happy hunting ground for the discriminating shopper.

❷ Farther along Brompton Road, on the right, is the **Brompton Oratory,** a very Italianate Roman Catholic church both inside and out, though lacking the sparkle and glamour of its southern counterparts.

❸ The next building is the **Victoria and Albert Museum,** clifflike and surmounted by cupolas, structured like a cross between a crown and a wedding cake. This is the heart of the South Kensington museum complex. It may seem strange that there can be two such museums as the British Museum and the V&A (as it's always called) in the same city, but they really do serve two different purposes. In some realms they overlap a little, as with drawings and watercolors, but the main function of the V&A is to act as a teaching museum, heavily committed to design from every age and country. As such it has an unrivaled collection in many spheres, and one can spend hours wandering through its endless rooms, surrounded on all sides by artistic treasures from France, Italy, the East and, of course, Britain itself. Have an idea of what you want to see and arm yourself with a free plan when you go in or you could quickly lose yourself in the endless maze.

The collection is so vast, and so rich, that it is difficult to pick out the most exciting elements. The paintings of Constable rank very high on any list; so do the jewel rooms, especially the massive Baroque jewels; the delicate miniatures, with some of the loveliest painted in Elizabeth I's reign; the medieval church art, with its elaborate workmanship and occasional glimpses into a world haunted by the fear of death and damnation; a profusion of Renaissance art, especially a series of magnificent Raphael cartoons loaned by the queen; costumes from many periods, excellently exhibited in the dress collection; musical instruments bewildering in their complexity and artisanship, and frequently played in fascinating recitals; Chinese, Islamic, and Indian art; Japanese art in a new gallery; the huge collection of sculpture reproductions . . . the list is endless. *Cromwell Rd., tel. 071/938–8500 or 071/938–8349 (recorded information). Admission free, but a £3.50 donation (£1 for children) is requested. Open Mon. noon–5:50, Tues.–Sun. 10–5:50; closed Good Friday, May Day, Dec. 24–26, Jan. 1.*

Next to the V&A come the museums devoted to science—the Natural History Museum and the Science Museum. The more spectacular, from ❹ the outside at any rate, is the **Natural History Museum,** a marvelous late-Victorian building by Alfred Waterhouse with ultramodern additions. Note the little animals carved into the cathedrallike entrance. The collections are excellent and very instructive for children, with dioramas and a massive, full-size model of a blue whale. The Earth Galleries feature an earthquake

Knightsbridge and Kensington

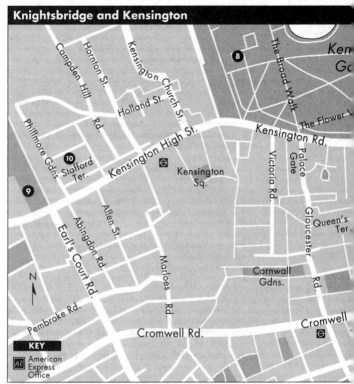

Campden Hill Rd.
Hornton St.
Kensington Church St.
Holland St.
Kensington High St.
Phillimore Gdns.
Stafford Ter.
Kensington Sq.
Allen St.
Abingdon Rd.
Earl's Court Rd.
Marloes Rd.
Pembroke Rd.
Cromwell Rd.
Kensington Rd.
The Broad Walk
The Flower
Victoria Rd.
Palace Gate
Gloucester Rd.
Queen's Ter.
Cornwall Gdns.
Cromwell
Ken Ga

KEY

AE American Express Office

Albert Memorial, **7**

Brompton Oratory, **2**

Commonwealth Institute, **9**

Harrods, **1**

Kensington Palace, **8**

Linley Sambourne House, **10**

Natural History Museum, **4**

Royal Albert Hall, **6**

Science Museum, **5**

Victoria and Albert Museum, **3**

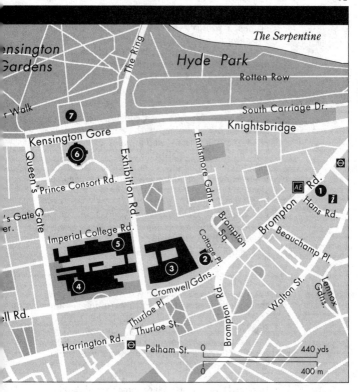

simulation center and a large collection of gemstones. *Cromwell Rd., tel. 071/938–9123. Admission: £4 adults, £2 children under 15, £2.30 senior citizens; family ticket (2 adults plus 4 children) £10.50. Admission free weekdays 4:30–6, weekends 5–6. Open Mon.–Sat. 10–6., Sun. 1–6; closed Good Friday, May Day, Dec. 24–26, Jan. 1.*

⑤ The **Science Museum** has consistently proved itself highly popular, with working models, changing exhibitions, and a policy of providing both instruction and fun for kids with a recently expanded "hands-on" exhibit area. An enormous range of topics is covered, from locomotives and computers to space technology and the history of medicine. *Exhibition Rd., tel. 071/938–8000 or 071/938–8008. Admission: £3.75 adults, £1.90 children aged 6–14, £2.20 senior citizens. Open Mon.–Sat. 10–6, Sun. 11–6; closed Good Friday, May Day, Dec. 24–26, Jan. 1.*

Exhibition Road, the wide thoroughfare that runs up north beside the V&A, will take you through the heart of this cultural complex—and that's exactly what it is and was planned to be by the serious Victorians, taking their cue from the pedagogical Prince Albert—and on to Kensington Gardens. On the right side of Exhibition Road is the large Mormon Chapel topped by a thin spike covered in gold leaf. On the left is the Imperial College of Science, now part of London University. At the center of the college campus is the **Queen's Tower,** all that remains of the Imperial Institute, which was demolished in the early 1960s after the Imperial Institute became the Commonwealth Institute (*see* Kensington, *below*), and moved to Holland Park. There is an uninterrupted view of London from the upper gallery, and displays relate the history of the tower; the belfry contains a peal of 10 bells. *Imperial College, Exhibition Rd., tel. 071/589–5111. The Tower has been closed to the public recently, but groups writing in advance may be able to arrange a tour.*

Prince Consort Road runs left off Exhibition Road. Above it stands the massive bulk of the **⑥** **Royal Albert Hall,** named for Victoria's consort and nowadays scene of the summer series of Promenade Concerts (known as the Proms) that have been running for nine healthy decades. These concerts, now sponsored by the BBC, form one of the most comprehensive festivals of music in the world. They last for eight weeks with a concert every day. The huge amphitheater, resplendent in wine-red and gold, is a truly Victorian temple to art and science. If you are not able to get to a concert, it is still worth wandering round the outside and across the road to look at the **Albert Memorial** and to walk into Kensington Gardens (*see below*). Beside the statue of Albert at the back of the hall—there are statues of Albert everywhere—are the restored **Royal College of Organists** (1875) and the modern **Royal College of Art,** where there are sometimes exhibitions worth seeing.

Kensington

The Royal Borough of Kensington and Chelsea, once *the* residential area of London, is now a very mixed bag. Most of the stately houses have been divided into apartments, but the feeling of stuccoed wealth, the pillared porches, and the tree-filled squares remain.

King William III, who suffered from asthma, found the Thames mists that frequently veiled Whitehall very trying. So in 1689 he bought Nottingham House, as it was then called, sited in the rural village of Kensington, where he was able to breathe more easily. Renamed Kensington Palace, and enlarged from time to time, it still acts as the spiritual heart of the neighborhood.

With the arrival of royalty the village "flourished almost beyond belief," according to a chronicler writing in 1705. Court functionaries hurried to follow the royal example, and **Kensington Square** (just behind the House of Fraser department store) was built to accommodate them. In the reign of Queen Anne (1702–14), the demand for lodging became so pressing that at one time an ambassador, a bishop, and a physician occupied apartments in the same house in the square.

Kensington Palace was greatly extended and improved by both the monarchs who subsequently lived here, the Hanoverians George I and George II. (The latter had the misfortune to die here while sitting on the toilet, though the public announcement had it that he was on the throne at the time.) On and off for more than a century, leading architects were employed in remodeling the palace, and their work is to be seen in those state apartments that are open to the public. It was here, too, that the young Princess Victoria was called from her bed on the night of June 20, 1837, by the Archbishop of Canterbury and the Lord Chamberlain, to be told of the death of her uncle, William IV, and her accession to the throne. Today the palace is the London home of Princess Margaret.

Some rooms in the **state apartments** are furnished as they were in the 1830s when the young Victoria lived out her restricted childhood with her domineering mother and governess. Visitors can also see the **Court Dress Collection,** which consists of "Ladies' and Gentlemen's Court Dress and Uniforms from 1750 to the 1950s" displayed in period settings. Both court dress and court behavior were governed by strict rules, and the exhibition opens this curious world of rigid etiquette to the public. *Kensington Gdns., tel. 071/937–9561. Admission: £3.75 adults, £2.50 children under 16, £2.80 senior citizens. Open Mon.–Sat. 9–5, Sun. 11–5; closed Good Friday, Dec. 24–26, Jan. 1.*

Immediately behind the palace runs **Kensington Palace Gardens** (called Palace Green at the south end), a wide and leafy avenue of large houses set in their own grounds and mostly the work of the leading architects of the 1850s and '60s. Thackeray, the novelist—author of *Vanity Fair*—died at #2 in 1863, in a house he had designed for himself. It is now the Israeli Embassy. This is one of the few private roads in London, with a uniformed guard at either end.

Just past the towering, modern Royal Garden Hotel is **Kensington Church Street,** which runs up to the right, with St. Mary Abbots Church on the corner. It looks genuinely medieval, but was built on the site of a much earlier church in the 1870s by Gilbert Scott, who also designed the Albert Memorial. This is rich territory for the antiques enthusiast. All the way up this winding road are shops specializing in everything from Japanese armor to Victorian commemorative china.

If you turn back down to Kensington High Street, now a busy shopping area, and follow it westward, you will come eventually to the **Commonwealth Institute.** You'll recognize it by the swimming-pool-blue walls and huge, tent-like copper roof. It stands back from the street in its own spacious grounds. Although the Commonwealth plays a much less important role in British affairs nowadays (just as British influence on other Commonwealth members has diminished), this institute is very much alive, with excellent, attractively displayed exhibits from the member countries, and frequent concerts and film shows. *230 Kensington High St., tel. 071/603-4535. Admission free. Open Mon.–Sat. 10–5, Sun. 2–5; closed Good Friday, Dec. 24–26, Jan. 1.*

On the eastern side of the Commonwealth Institute is the **Linley Sambourne House,** a little masterpiece of Victoriana. Managed by the Victorian Society, this fascinating survival was sold intact to the City of London by the Countess of Rosse, mother of Lord Snowdon and the granddaughter of the man who built and furnished the place in the 1870s, Edward Linley Sambourne. For over 30 years, Linley Sambourne was the main political cartoonist for the satirical magazine *Punch.* For anyone interested in the Victorian era, a visit here is a must. *18 Stafford Terr., tel. 081/994-1019. Admission: £2 adults, £1 children under 16. Open Mar.–Oct., Wed. 10–4, Sun. 2–5.*

Hyde Park and Kensington Gardens

Numbers in the margin correspond to points of interest on the Hyde Park and Kensington Gardens map.

The Royal Parks are among London's unique features: Great swathes of green in the middle of the city, where it really is possible to escape from the noise and urgency of the metropolis. The description "royal" is somewhat paradoxical, for today these are the most democratic of places, where Londoners of every class and background come to relax. Yet the parks owe their very survival to monarchical origins. Having first been established as places where royalty hunted, walked, or rode, they acquired a privileged status and remained immune from the greedy clutches of property developers during London's many phases of expansion.

This section describes a walk through the two largest Royal Parks in central London. Hyde Park and Kensington Gardens are technically separate, but on the ground it is impossible to know where one stops and the other begins. **Hyde Park** covers 361 acres, stretching from the Bayswater Road in the north to Knightsbridge in the south and bounded by Park Lane in the east. To the west lies Kensington Gardens, another 273 acres, once the private grounds of Kensington Palace, but now the continuation of Hyde Park; together the two areas form the largest open space in central London. Both parks have fine trees—though many were badly damaged or destroyed in the terrible storm of October 1987—plus some attractive areas of flower beds, seasonally replanted, and a surprisingly large variety of birds.

Though there are gates all around the park, most of them splendidly decorative, the main ❶ entrance to Hyde Park is **Decimus Burton's Gateway** at the southern end of Park Lane, just ❷ by **Apsley House** (*see* St. James's and Mayfair, *above*). To the left, as you enter, is **Rotten Row,** a long avenue that runs along the bottom of the park. It's a sandy track with paths on each side that used to be a popular strolling place, especially on Sundays after church. Today it is used almost exclusively for riding. The odd name is an English corruption of *route du roi,* for this was the route taken by the king's carriage when going from Whitehall to Kensington Palace.

Henry VIII was the first monarch to use the area as a royal hunting ground, and deer roamed the park until the middle of the last century. Charles I transformed it into a place where fashionable society could see and be seen; a circular drive was laid out for carriages to parade around. Later the park became a locality for duels. In 1851 the first Great International Exhibition was held here in the magnificent surroundings of the specially constructed Crystal Palace.

3 Heading into the center of the park from Apsley House, you will come across the statue of **Achilles,** standing 20 feet high. This was yet another tribute to Wellington, paid for by subscriptions from the admiring women of Britain. The assembled ladies must have had a shock when this colossal nude, cast from the metal of guns captured during some of the duke's famous victories, was finally unveiled in 1822.

Farther along is the start of a long, man-made, crescent-shaped lake called the **Serpentine** in Hyde Park and the **Long Water** in Kensington Gardens. The poet Shelley's abandoned first wife, Harriet Westbrook, drowned herself here in 1816 when she was pregnant.

Strolling along the edge of the Serpentine is one of the most enjoyably near-rural pleasures that London has to offer. At any season of the year the lake has its own atmosphere: In summer it's almost a seaside scene, the grass strewn with deck chairs and the water busy with boats; in winter it takes on an air of gentle melancholy, the trees sketching bare traceries against the gray sky, the water visited by swooping gulls.

4 Past the swimming area you will arrive at the **Serpentine Bridge,** which carries the main road across the park. This is an elegant structure, built in 1826, which looks like a stage set come to life among the trees, especially at night. From here you get a good view of Westminster's skyline to the southeast.

Once across the bridge you are in **Kensington Gardens.** These began as the private grounds of Kensington Palace, and were landscaped by Queen Caroline, wife of George II, who created most of their present features. Just south of the **5** bridge is the **Serpentine Gallery,** an art gallery that houses regular exhibitions, usually of interesting modern works. *Kensington Gdns., tel.*

Hyde Park and Kensington Gardens

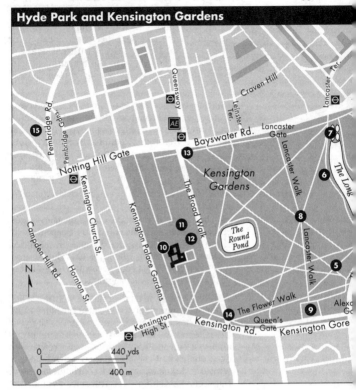

Achilles, **3**	Peter Pan, **6**
Albert Memorial, **9**	Physical Energy, **8**
Apsley House, **2**	Portobello Road, **15**
Black Lion Gate, **13**	Serpentine Bridge, **4**
Decimus Burton's Gateway, **1**	Serpentine Gallery, **5**
The Fountains, **7**	Sunken Garden, **11**
Kensington Palace, **10**	
Orangery, **12**	
Palace Gate, **14**	

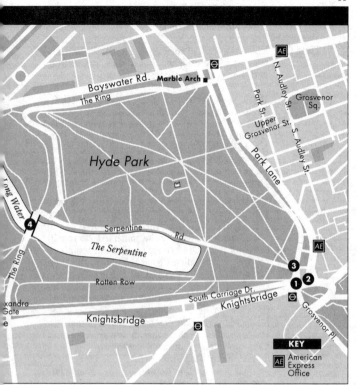

071/402–6075. Admission free. Open daily 10–6; closed Christmas week.

Time Out   The restaurant at the eastern end of the Serpentine offers sandwiches, hot dishes, tea, coffee, and snacks in a very attractive location.

If you walk northward along the western (left) bank of the Long Water, you will pass the statue **⑥** of **Peter Pan,** who was supposed to live on an island in the Serpentine. His creator, J.M. Barrie, had a house just north of the park, at 100 Bayswater Road. At the end of the lake you will **⑦** reach a paved Italianate garden called **The Fountains.**

The southwesterly walkway from here will take you past an obelisk memorial to the explorer J.H. Speke, who discovered the source of the Nile. **Lancaster Walk** to the south from here will lead you to a huge bronze equestrian sculpture **⑧** by G.F. Watts called **Physical Energy,** and then **⑨** on to the **Albert Memorial,** at the southern extreme of the gardens. This monument—the expression of Queen Victoria's obsessive reverence for her dead husband's memory—was for many years considered the ugliest landmark in the country. Tastes change, however, and many have developed a quiet affection for this "memorial of our Blameless Prince." You may have trouble seeing the details of the memorial, though, as it is badly eroded by air pollution, and often surrounded by scaffolding or hoardings, while experts decide how to preserve it.

From just above the memorial, **Flower Walk** angles westward. The long flower beds bloom for most of the year, with the displays being regularly changed. At the end of the Flower Walk the **⑩** **Broad Walk** bisects the gardens, and beyond it stands **Kensington Palace** (*see* Knightsbridge and Kensington, *above*).

⑪ Northeast of the palace is a **Sunken Garden,** dating from 1909 and surrounded by lime trees, and **⑫** an **Orangery,** which was built two centuries earlier. On the other side of the Broad Walk from the palace is the **Round Pond,** a favorite spot for ducks, pigeons, and model yachtsmen. The Broad Walk leads north to the Bayswater Road

⓭ through the **Black Lion Gate,** while to the south
⓮ it leads to Kensington Road via the **Palace
Gate.**

Black Lion Gate is only a few minutes' walk
away from **Notting Hill,** a lively residential
quarter with some interesting bookshops, art
galleries, and antiques shops. Behind the main
⓯ road lies **Portobello Road,** where the Saturday
market is a magnet for every antiques-hunter in
London. It's essential to arrive early for the
best choice—but at even at the busiest times the
hunt will be fun, and you might be able to un-
cover some good buys. The regular antiques
dealers along Portobello Road and in the neighboring streets are normally open on weekdays.

Time Out   Two pâtisseries near the north side of Kensington Gardens are **Maison Pechon** (127 Queens-
way) and, slightly more expensive, **Maison
Bouquillon** (41 Moscow Rd.). Hot chocolate,
strong coffee, and fresh-baked croissants and
pastries are specialties of both establishments.

Soho and Covent Garden

*Numbers in the margin correspond to points of
interest on the Soho and Covent Garden map.*

Once London's red-light district, Soho these
days is more stylish than seedy. It has the unusual distinction of being one of the very few
areas of London whose borders are quite clear.
It also has the distinction of being laid out on the
nearest thing to a grid plan that London has to
offer, which makes this, the most concentrated
and international district of London's West
End, a pretty easy place to get around. Soho's
unusual name is believed to derive from the days
when this was hunting land attached to the
nearby Palace of Westminster, "So-Ho!" being a
common hunting cry of the time.

Soho has always had a substantial immigrant
population. The first foreigners to settle here
were Greeks escaping from Turkish oppression,

and French Huguenots (Protestants) fleeing Catholic oppression in their homeland. Later waves of French came after the revolutionary upheavals at the end of the 18th century and the Paris Commune of 1870. In fact, one of Soho's most celebrated restaurants, Wheelers in Old Compton Street, was started by one of Napoleon's chefs. Many famous refugees and temporary visitors to London have lived in this area, including Karl Marx, Wagner, and Haydn.

Today, the predominant foreign influences are Italian and Chinese. The Italian influence is apparent almost everywhere in Soho, but the Chinese community is gathered in only one corner, around pedestrianized Gerrard Street, to the south of Shaftesbury Avenue. Here, a cluster of Chinese restaurants and supermarkets, Chinese-style phone boxes, a pair of pagoda arches, and other street decorations combine to create London's mini version of Chinatown.

Soho owes its slightly exotic air to the cosmopolitan nature of the people it has welcomed within its borders, an air that makes it subtly, but distinctly, different from the rest of staid, insular London. In addition to the film, record, and advertising companies, restaurateurs, and other high-profile folk who have made this their natural territory, it should be no surprise that Soho also has traditionally attracted members of the oldest profession. This was never a situation that local residents have been happy about, and several clean-up campaigns have greatly altered matters, though some strip clubs, a few soft-porn movie houses, and several fairly discreet sex shops remain.

You can choose practically any point from which to launch an expedition into Soho; it's not a large area and all the most interesting points are easily reached. Given that there's no ideal point from which to start—and because you've got to start somewhere—our description of Soho begins at **Oxford Circus,** which, if nothing else, is very easy to find.

Head south down Regent Street a couple of hundred yards from Oxford Circus and make a left into Great Marlborough Street. This leads you ❶ past the black-and-white facade of **Liberty** department store to the north end of **Carnaby Street.** Carnaby Street's dizzy heyday as a fashion and pop music mecca back in the Swinging Sixties evaporated almost entirely without a trace many years ago, though today's pedestrian-only street and the surrounding area—revived, refitted, and remarketed as "West Soho"—has undergone a revival. The small network of lanes off to the left harbor several interesting little crafts shops, among them the **Craftsmen Potters Shop** on parallel Marshall Street, and a cluster of high-fashion young designers' emporia in and around Broadwick Street.

The Romantic poet and painter William Blake was born at #74 Broadwick Street in 1758. This street leads to Berwick (pronounced "Berik") Street, scene of a thriving daily market. Pick your way past the crowded stalls, trying not to slip on the squashed cabbage leaves, to reach Old Compton Street. This is one of Soho's major thoroughfares—the other is Wardour Street—famed for, in about equal measure, its cafés, restaurants, and sex shops.

Attractions lie to both the north and the south. To the north, up Frith Street, is the prettiest and probably the most interesting square in the area, **Soho Square.** It was laid out in about 1680 and became fashionable in the 18th century; only two of the original buildings are left. The garden in the middle is distinguished for the tiny cottage that seems to come straight out of Disney's *Snow White*—it's actually a toolshed that was put up in the last century. At the corner of Soho Square and Greek Street is **St. Barnabas-in-Soho,** a charitable institution whose fine 18th-century house is open to the public. The plasterwork, staircases, and fireplaces are well worth a look. *1 Greek St., tel. 071/437–1894. Open Wed. 2:30–4, Thurs. 11–12:30.*

The next street over, Dean Street, runs south into Shaftesbury Avenue, which effectively divides Soho from the Chinese area based around Gerrard Street. Shaftesbury Avenue is the heart of London's theaterland.

74

Soho and Covent Garden

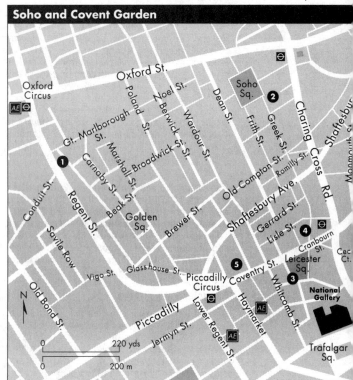

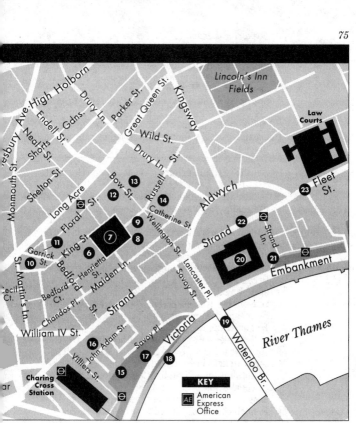

KEY

AE American Express Office

Time Out The area just above Shaftesbury Avenue is a good place for tea shops (or *pâtisseries*, since they are mostly of French origin). Two worth sampling are **Maison Bertaux** (28 Greek St.) and, just around the corner, **Pâtisserie Valerie** (44 Old Compton St.). Prices aren't low, but the cakes are delicious (some of the stickiest and creamiest in London) and the cafés are a good place to watch the world go by.

South of Shaftesbury Avenue and Gerrard Street is **Leicester** (pronounced "Lester") **Square.** It's among the oldest and most famous of London's squares, having been laid out originally as early as 1630. By the 19th century it had gained a reputation as a place of slightly disreputable theaters, restaurants, and dance halls. It still performs its traditional role as an entertainment center, though now its theaters have become cinemas and its dance halls discos. Despite its faint hint of Times Square, it remains a reasonably likable place. There are statues of Shakespeare and Charles Chaplin, the artists Hogarth and Reynolds, and an invisible new £22 million electrical substation underfoot. On the ❸ southwest corner is the **Society of West End Theatres' ticket kiosk,** where you can buy half-price tickets for many London theaters on the day of the performance. Leicester Place, on the northeast corner of Leicester Square, contains the ❹ French church of **Notre Dame de France.** One of the side chapels is decorated with a mural by the great French artist and poet Jean Cocteau.

Also off the west side is the **Trocadero Centre**—an entertainment complex with shops and the ❺ **Guinness World of Records,** a three-dimensional re-creation of the odd and amazing facts and figures, records and achievements, catalogued in the world-famous *Guinness Book of World Records. Guinness World of Records, Trocadero, tel. 071/439–7331. Admission: £5 adults, £3.20 children under 15, £3.95 senior citizens. Open daily 10–10. Closed Christmas.*

Just beyond the Trocadero is Piccadilly Circus (*see* St. James's and Mayfair, *above*).

Cranbourn Street, at the northeast corner of
Leicester Square, will lead you to Charing
Cross Road, the eastern border of Soho, laid out
like Shaftesbury Avenue in the 19th century.
Heading left (north) up Charing Cross Road you
pass a series of new and secondhand bookstores.
Just above busy Cambridge Circus is #84, which
gave the title to Helen Hanff's memorable book
(subsequently a movie). It's now a record store.

Finally, though not strictly speaking in Soho,
you might like to explore the little courts and al-
leyways running off the Charing Cross Road,
among them **Cecil Court** and **Bedford Court**.
They are lined with print shops, secondhand
bookstores, and some record stores. This is the
place to find old theatrical posters, programs,
and books on every subject under the sun. It is
also an excellent area for pubs. Try the **Salis-
bury,** the **Black Horse,** or the wonderfully
named **Green Man and French Horn** on St. Martin's Lane, just across from the end of Cecil
Court.

Covent Garden

St. Martin's Lane makes a convenient point
from which to head into Covent Garden. Or, if
you plan to explore Covent Garden without having first been to Soho, just take the tube to Covent Garden station. In any event, you should
begin your exploration of this ever-more-charac-
terful chunk of central London at the born-again
old **Covent Garden Market.**

Originally, the "Convent Garden" belonged to
the 13th-century Abbey of St. Peter at Westminster, for which it produced fruit and vegetables. Following the dissolution of the monaster-
ies in the mid-16th century, the Crown took
possession of the lands and awarded them in
1552 to John Russell, first earl of Bedford. In
1630 the fourth earl (later the duke of Bedford—
dukes outrank earls) commissioned Inigo Jones,
the leading architect of the day, who also designed the Banqueting House on Whitehall, to
lay out a square on the site. **St. Paul's Church**
was at one end, tall, elegantly colonnaded
houses lined the north and east sides, and the
plain rear wall of Bedford House (the earl's Lon-

don residence) filled the south side. This was the first of London's great squares, and it influenced the design and construction of many later ones. Sadly, of the original buildings, only the church remains today.

With the opening of Westminster Bridge in the mid-18th century, Covent Garden became well established and grew to be one of the world's foremost fruit, vegetable, and flower markets. However, after World War II, as the market expanded, it became clear that the surrounding narrow streets and buildings were acting as a straitjacket to development and creating the most appalling traffic jams. And so, in 1974, market operations were moved to a new site at Nine Elms, south of the Thames, leaving the deserted Covent Garden ripe for redevelopment. The area was very nearly turned into yet another jungle of glass-and-concrete high-rise office blocks, but after a prolonged protest campaign, a plan of small-scale development was adopted, which has generally been very successful.

At the heart of Covent Garden is the market building itself, overlooked by the back of St. Paul's, whose main entrance is on Bedford Street. St. Paul's is a rather stark church, inside and out, but worth visiting for the memorials to famous theater folk that line the walls. It is popularly known as "the actors' church." The portico facing the market building provides an excellent stage for open-air entertainment—jazz musicians, jugglers, fire-eaters, and mime troupes.

❼ The **market building** is the centerpiece of the whole area, and was built for the Duke of Bedford in 1840. Following the move of the vegetable and fruit markets to Nine Elms, it was carefully restored and reopened in 1980, having been converted into an unusual shopping center, with boutiques and crafts shops, health-food bars, and gift shops galore. On its south side is the lively and much less formal Jubilee market, catering to artists and artisans and selling clothing, records, toys, and a multitude of flea-market goods. The best time to visit it for crafts is on the weekend. There are plenty of restaurants and cafés nearby, or, if you just need to rest your legs, you can sit on the steps and watch the people go by.

On the southeastern corner of the square stands the old Flower Market, now the **London Transport Museum.** It contains an extensive collection of vehicles, including an original omnibus, trains (including a steam locomotive used on the Underground as long ago as 1866), trams, and buses. This is a real "hands-on" museum, and you are encouraged to try out many of the exhibits, which makes it a popular place with children. *39 Wellington St., tel. 071/379–6344. Admission: usually £3.20 adults, £1.60 children 5–16 and senior citizens, children under 5 free; but the museum is closed for refurbishment as we go to press. Call for new opening hours and admission prices.*

The long-awaited **Theatre Museum** opened in 1987 next door on Shakespeare's birthday, April 23. It is devoted to the British theater from Shakespeare to the present day in all its many facets—not merely straight drama, but also musical comedy, opera, rock and pop, circus, pantomime, and music hall (vaudeville). The main exhibition contains theatrical memorabilia of every kind, including prints and paintings of the earliest London theaters, early play scripts, costumes, and props. The Paintings Gallery, designed in the style of an ornate theater foyer, contains a collection of paintings of performers in character. There is a well-stocked bookshop, a box office that sells seats for all the main London theaters, and an attractive café. *1E Tavistock St., tel. 071/836–7891. Admission: £3 adults, £1.50 children aged 5–14 and senior citizens. Open Tues.–Sun. 11–7; closed Mon., Good Friday, Dec. 24–26, Jan. 1.*

The streets leading away from the market building, into and around the rest of Covent Garden, are equally intriguing. To the north—walk up James Street past the back of the Royal Opera House—is **Long Acre,** running east/west. A way down to your left is **Dillons Arts Bookshop,** a good bet for books, posters, and postcards; and, nearly next door, **Stanfords** has the best collection of travel books, guidebooks, and maps in town.

Turn left again at the end of Long Acre into Garrick Street. On the right is the grave facade of ❿ the **Garrick Club,** one of the city's best-known gentlemen's clubs. It's famous today as an actors' club (Laurence Olivier was one of the longest-serving members), though Dickens, Thackeray, and Trollope all belonged to it in their day. Rose Street is a tiny alley on the left, ⓫ at the end of which is the **Lamb and Flag,** one of London's few remaining authentic Dickensian pubs.

To get back to the heart of Covent Garden from Garrick Street, walk down the narrow passage by the side of the Lamb and Flag pub and turn right along Floral Street, which will bring you back to James Street. From here, continue north across Long Acre, into Neal Street, or turn right onto Long Acre.

Neal Street, half of which is open to pedestrians only, is full of little shops, restaurants, and crafts galleries. The **Contemporary Applied Arts building,** a block up on the left on the corner of Earlham Street, has regular exhibits of pottery, jewelry, and textiles. Some items are for sale, though they can be expensive.

If instead of taking Neal Street you turn right down Long Acre, you will come to the **Glasshouse** where all day long you can watch glassblowers practicing their craft and purchase any piece that catches your eye. **Bow Street** will then be on the right. It is known for two things: the Royal Opera House and, practically opposite it, the Magistrates' Court.

⓬ The present theater, today the **Royal Opera House,** opened in 1858. There had been two previous theaters here since the 18th century. The first, built in 1732, burned down in 1808, a common theatrical event in the days before electricity. Its replacement suffered the same fate in 1856. The existing theater then became England's principal opera house, and adopted its present name in 1936. In 1956 its two resident companies, the Sadler's Wells Ballet and the Covent Garden Opera Company, became the Royal Ballet and the Royal Opera Company, respectively. The rear of the building was extended in 1981—at a huge cost—providing much needed rehearsal space and dressing rooms. The theater's atmosphere and acoustics are superb, with the rich Victorian gilt decorations and plush seats setting off performances to their best advantage.

❶ **Bow Street Magistrates' Court** was established in 1740 by Colonel Thomas de Veil, who was succeeded in 1749 by Henry Fielding (1707–54), a noted magistrate, but also a journalist and the prolific author of *Tom Jones* and *Joseph Andrews.* Fielding employed a band of private detectives, the "Bow Street Runners," and paid them out of the fines that were imposed in the court. In 1829, the Home Secretary, Sir Robert Peel, formed the first regular police force—thus creating the first British "bobby." The force was based at #4 Whitehall, backing onto a courtyard known as Scotland Yard, but it was only in 1879 that a police station was established next to the Magistrates' Court in Bow Street; it closed in early 1993.

❷ Head down Bow Street and turn left into Russell Street. Straight ahead you'll see the **Theatre Royal, Drury Lane,** the largest theater in London, and probably the most famous. It's the fourth theater built on this site, the original dating from 1660.

The Strand and Embankment

To the south of Covent Garden is **The Strand,** one of London's most historic streets, though today little more than a broad thoroughfare lined with office blocks and shops. Its historic significance lies in the vital role it used to play as the main route between the City to the northeast and Westminster. Its name comes simply from the fact that originally it was a "strand," or beach, along the banks of the Thames. With the building of the parallel Victoria Embankment along the north bank of the Thames in the 1870s, the Strand lost its links with London's great river, and its historic role disappeared with the arrival of alternate routes to the City. From the 15th to the 17th century this stretch of riverbank was the site of some of London's most aristocratic houses, though the only reminder now of those

❸ palmy days is the **York Watergate** at the western

end of the Victoria Embankment Gardens. Built in about 1625, it was the river entrance to the Duke of Buckingham's mansion, York House. In those days, before the Victoria Embankment was built, this watergate was actually on the Thames.

Down at the south end of the Strand is **Charing Cross Station,** one of London's main train stations. A 19th-century copy of an elaborate medieval memorial-cum-cross stands outside it. The original was put up by the 13th-century king Edward I to mark the resting place of the coffin of his wife, Eleanor, on its way to her funeral at Westminster Abbey.

Between the Strand and the river, just beyond Charing Cross Station, is the area called the **Adelphi,** built in the late 18th century by the Scottish architect brothers, John and Robert Adam. Though most of their elegant brick town houses have since been knocked down, enough remain to give a taste of the days when the "People of Quality" flocked to live here (look especially at those on Adam Street).

Behind the Adelphi is the **Victoria Embankment Gardens,** a quiet haven where many office workers spend their lunch hour in the summer. The flower beds are beautifully kept, while the shrubs and trees filter the noise of the Embankment traffic. The gardens are interesting also for the statues they contain, including one to Robert Burns, who sits on a tree stump being inspired by his muse.

Fronting the gardens is the **Victoria Embankment,** laid out between 1868 and 1874 by the indefatigable Sir Joseph Bazalgette, otherwise best remembered as the man who built London's sewers (almost all of them still functioning, though beginning to show signs of wear). Running from Westminster to the City, its bold engineering and ornate cast-iron street lamps became the talk of London.

The principal point of interest now on the Victoria Embankment is **Cleopatra's Needle,** a weathered pink granite obelisk that has no connection whatsoever with Cleopatra. It is the oldest out-of-doors object of any kind in London by a clear

1,000 years or more. Some of the seats along this stretch of the Embankment carry on the Egyptian theme, with camels as supports.

⑲ Continuing eastward, **Waterloo Bridge** provides one of the best river viewpoints in London—around the bend of the Thames in both directions to the City and to Westminster. And from here also you get the best view of the spectacular 18th-century facade of **Somerset House,** the **⑳** new home of the **Courtauld Institute Galleries,** on the Strand east of Waterloo Bridge. Until the Victoria Embankment was built in the last century, the Thames at high tide lapped at the foot of the building, adding greatly to its charm, as contemporary pictures make clear. Until 1973, Somerset House was headquarters of the Registrar General of Births, Deaths, and Marriages, and also contained a number of other government offices. Today, the magnificent Courtauld collections of the art of the Old Masters and the French Impressionists have been transferred to the stately public rooms of Somerset House. *The Strand, tel. 071/873–2526. Admission: £3 adults, £1.50 children, students, and senior citizens. Open Mon.–Sat. 10–6, Sun. 2–6. Closed public holidays.*

Next door to Somerset House, in Strand Lane, **㉑** is the so-called **Roman Bath.** It probably dates from the 17th century, rather than from Roman times. Nonetheless, it is thought that the Romans knew and used the spring that feeds the bath. It is owned by the National Trust today, and can be viewed from a pathway.

Opposite Somerset House lies the **Aldwych,** a substantial crescent (curved, Georgian street) containing three theaters and the massive **Bush House,** the home of the BBC World Service. The eastern end of the island formed by the Aldwych and the Strand is occupied by **Australia House,** the London headquarters of the Commonwealth of Australia.

This end of the Strand is graced by two of London's prettiest churches, both forming unusual little islands in the middle of the road. The most westerly, almost opposite Somerset **㉒** House, is **St. Mary-le-Strand,** an attractive early 18th-century church designed by James Gibbs.

㉓ The other, more easterly, church is **St. Clement Danes,** designed by Wren, with a tower added later by Gibbs, and containing the tuneful bells that provided the inspiration for the nursery rhyme "Oranges and lemons, say the bells of St. Clement's." Inside there's a statue of Dr. Johnson, once a regular worshipper here. Today St. Clement's is the principal church of the RAF, the Royal Air Force, and guards a book containing the names of 1,900 American airmen killed during World War II. St. Clement's is an excellent example of imaginative restoration.

The City

Numbers in the margin correspond to points of interest on the City map.

The City of London is nothing if not confusingly named. Mention it to most Britons and they'll assume you're talking about the great financial institutions based here, always collectively referred to as "the City," the British version of Wall Street. Mention it to most visitors and the odds are they'll just think you mean London as a whole. In fact, the City (note the capital letter) is a distinct and precise area of London. Much more than just another district, it is an administrative and legal entity in itself, in many important respects quite separate from the rest of London.

Often called the Square Mile (though it is neither square nor a mile in area), the City lies to the east of central London, stretching from the Temple Bar at its western border to the Tower of London in the east, and from Smithfield in the north to the Thames in the south. Its 677 acres are jammed with a multitude of buildings both ancient and modern. Yet though it is crowded by day, at night an almost ghostly emptiness pervades its ancient streets. Its permanent population numbers fewer than 8,000.

Temple Bar to Ludgate Hill

❶ The main gateway to the City is **Temple Bar** in Fleet Street. Its significance stems from the fact that it was this western approach that was the most direct route for travel to and from

Westminster and the City. But its curious name is misleading. First, there's no temple here. The term refers to the nearby Temple area. Second, there is no bar, and there hasn't been since 1870, when the handsome Baroque gateway built by Wren in 1670 was dismantled as an obstruction to traffic. Even this wasn't really a bar, but a ceremonial entryway. Today, a bronze griffin, emblem of the City, marks the site where Wren's gateway stood (similar griffins mark all the traditional entries to the City). It is here that by ancient custom the monarch must ask permission of the Lord Mayor of London to enter the City.

Fleet Street itself follows the course of the little river Fleet, which runs from Hampstead, where Fleet Road marks its course, to the Thames. There's no trace of it today, and hasn't been since 1765, when it was diverted into an underground pipe and boarded over. The fame of Fleet Street derives from its traditional role as the center of Britain's newspaper business. Today, spiraling rents and labor costs have forced all the newspapers away from Fleet Street, many of them having relocated to the massive redevelopment areas around London's docklands.

Halfway along Fleet Street, on its north side, turn down narrow Bolt Lane and follow the winding alley to **Dr. Johnson's House** in Gough Square. Here, in a 17th-century house, the writer lived in the 1750s while he was compiling his great dictionary. *17 Gough Sq., tel. 071/353–3745. Admission: £2 adults, £1.50 children under 16 and senior citizens. Open May–Sept., Mon.–Sat. 11–5:30; Oct.–Apr., Mon.–Sat. 11–5; closed national holidays.*

Around the corner from Gough Square, in Wine Office Court, is the **Cheshire Cheese** pub, with its historic beams and ancient fireplaces. This also dates from the 17th century, and was a favorite watering hole of Dr. Johnson and Boswell, his biographer and companion.

On the south side of Fleet Street stands **St. Bride,** built by Wren after the Norman church (where Pilgrim father Edward Winslow's par-

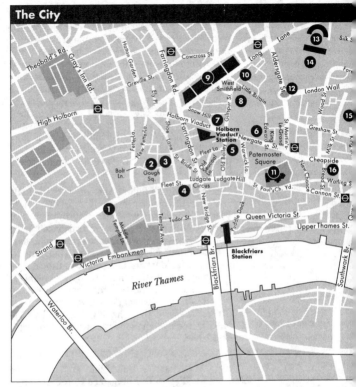

The City

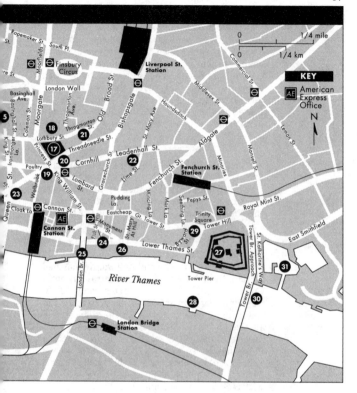

ents were married) was lost to the Great Fire. It was badly damaged in a 1940 air raid, restored over a 17-year period, and rededicated in 1960. The crypts were used for centuries as burial chambers and charnel house; they got a little crowded, as Samuel Pepys found in 1664, when he had to bribe the gravedigger to "justle together" some bodies to make room for his deceased brother. Now the crypts house a museum of the church's rich history. *Fleet St., tel. 071/ 353–1301. Admission free. Open Mon.–Sat. 9–5, Sun. between the services at 11 and 6:30.*

At the foot of Fleet Street is **Ludgate Circus,** a drab traffic circle which gets its name from the Lud Gate, believed to have been built in 66 BC by King Lud, who is today also commemorated by the **Old King Lud** pub on the corner. Ahead of you now is Ludgate Hill and St. Paul's.

Fleet Street runs into **Old Bailey,** at the northern end of which stood one of London's grisly prisons, Newgate. The building was demolished **❺** in 1902 to make way for the **Central Criminal Court,** or the Old Bailey as it is commonly called. The imposing Edwardian building, extended in the 1970s, is famous mainly for the gilt statue of Justice on the dome: the blindfolded figure impassively holding the scales and sword of justice in her hands. To watch a trial, head for courts 1–3, the old courts, where the juiciest trials usually take place. Courts 4–19 are modern, with restricted view from all but the front seats. *Public Gallery open weekdays 10–1, 2–4; the line forms at the Newgate St. entrance. Check the day's hearings on the sign outside.*

Continuing north from Old Bailey, turn right onto Newgate Street, then left on to King **❻** Edward Street. **The National Postal Museum** is an essential stop for philatelists and a curiosity for the rest of us. Housed in the General Post Office, this is one of the world's most important collections of postage stamps. The museum was founded in 1965, but the collections are as old as the postal service itself; there are also philatelic archives and an extensive reference library. *King Edward Bldg., King Edward St., tel. 071/ 239–5420. Admission free. Open Mon.–Thurs.*

9:30–4:30, Fri. 9:30–4; closed weekends, na-tional holidays.

From the museum, turn right on Newgate Street and then head up Giltspur Street. Immediately on the left here is the church of **St. Sepulchre-without-Newgate.** It is the resting place of Captain John Smith, "sometime Governor of Virginia and Admiral of New England," whose life was saved by Pocahontas.

A little farther up Giltspur Street, to the right, is **St. Bartholomew's Hospital,** one of the oldest charitable foundations in London and today a leading teaching hospital. It dates back to 1123. Though originally a monastic foundation, it was spared by Henry VIII in the 16th century when he so rigorously suppressed the country's other monastic foundations. Appropriately, there is a statue of him in the niche above the main gateway. (At press time, the hospital was under serious threat of closure.)

Just to the northwest of St. Bart's, as the hospital is called, is **Smithfield,** London's main meat market. The area has been a market of sorts since the 12th century, when this grassy spot (or "Smoothfield") just outside the then City walls was used as a horse market. In the mid-1800s the area was notorious for its stench and filth and for the drunkenness of the traders. The Victorians put a stop to all that when they built a new market in 1868, and banned the sale and slaughter of live animals. Following a fire after World War II, the market was again rebuilt, reopening in 1963.

Time Out   **Rudland and Stubbs** (35–37 Greenhill Rents) is a friendly fish restaurant in the heart of the meat market; you can lunch at the bar on fishy snacks or eat in style in the restaurant. The **Hand and Shears** (1 Middle St.) offers traditional pub food to City workers; watch for the lurid pub sign.

Just to the east of Smithfield is the church of **St. Bartholomew the Great,** the second-oldest church in London. It was founded, like its namesake the hospital, in 1123 by the Normans. The church is approached through an attractive gateway with an Elizabethan half-timbered facade. For many years this was covered by plaster, coming to light unexpectedly in 1915 when a bomb from a German zeppelin blew the plaster off. The interior of the church has undergone considerable rebuilding and restoration over the years, notably in the 16th and 19th centuries, leaving the choir as the only remaining section of the original Norman building. It possesses a monumental charm, not unlike the Chapel of St. John in the White Tower in the Tower of London. The church is often used for concerts, and to hear Bach or Handel performed in such surroundings can be a memorable experience.

St. Paul's Cathedral

Backtracking to Ludgate Hill, turn and walk up toward **St. Paul's.** Built by Sir Christopher Wren between 1675 and 1710, this building replaced the earlier Gothic cathedral that had stood here since the Middle Ages until it was destroyed in the Great Fire of 1666. The building is Wren's greatest work, and its instantly recognizable dome dominated the skyline for centuries, until insensitive modern developers began to surround it with trite towers. Fittingly, the architect himself is buried in the crypt, under the simple epitaph composed by his son: *Lector, si monumentum requiris, circumspice*—Reader, if you seek his monument, look around you.

Despite its vast size—520 feet long and 365 feet from the crown of the lantern on the dome to the ground—the church was built in the relatively short time of 35 years, which accounts for its unusually unified quality. Wren himself, well aware of the parsimony of his paymasters, can claim much of the credit for this. He insisted that all the foundations be laid from the start, thus ensuring that the dimensions of the building could not subsequently be altered. Equally striking is the consistently high level of craftsmanship, both inside and out. For the interior, Wren was very lucky to have the services of the great Dutch wood carver, Grinling Gibbons. His exquisitely carved choir stalls are particularly fine, as are the black-and-gold wrought iron screens by the French master, Jean Tijou.

Wren's designs for the building went through three distinct stages. His original plan was rejected, but the second, later called the Great Model, reached the stage of having a massive and beautifully detailed wooden model made of it, which is now on display in the crypt. The third design, or the Warrant Design as it came to be known, was the one finally chosen. But Wren made significant alterations to it during its construction, notably the substitution of a dome for the giant steeple he had originally designed. The construction of the dome itself was a difficult technical undertaking, with an elaborate brick cone built between the inner and outer skins to strengthen and support both. The interior of the dome presents another curiosity. Words whispered from one side of the aptly named **Whispering Gallery** can be clearly heard on the other side, 112 feet away. It's worth climbing the spiral steps to the Whispering Gallery, not only for the chance to test the remarkable acoustics, but also for the view down to the chancel and the nave. More steps climb up from the Whispering Gallery to the exterior **Stone Gallery,** some 70 feet above the Whispering Gallery, and then higher still to the **Golden Gallery** just below the lantern, ball, and cross. This last series of steps is very steep and, though quite safe, should not be attempted by the fainthearted. From bottom to top you will have climbed 627 steps! There are good views from both the Stone and Golden Galleries across the City and beyond. Try to pick out the distinctive steeples of Wren's many other City churches, and imagine the view in his time, centuries before the development of high-rises, when St. Paul's dominated the City skyline. These galleries are also good spots from which to study more closely the details of Wren's unusual and imaginative design; there are close views to be had of the flying buttresses and western towers, and you can see the brick cone that divides the inner and outer dome while you are on the steps leading up to the Golden Gallery.

The interior of the church is crowded with memorials, some indifferent, some good, almost all of them large and elaborate. Dr. Johnson; John Donne, the poet and dean of St. Paul's, whose effigy, wrapped in its shroud, is the only one to have survived the destruction of the Gothic cathedral; the artists Reynolds and Turner (in Painters' Corner); and the statesmen Wellington and George Washington are among those commemorated. One of the most impressive memorials is the American Memorial Chapel in the area behind the high altar (there's an admission charge). This chapel was dedicated in 1958 to the 28,000 Americans stationed in Britain who lost their lives in active service during World War II. The Roll of Honor was presented to St. Paul's by General Eisenhower in 1951. The walls are decorated with carvings of plants and birds indigenous to the United States. Henry Moore's sculpture *Mother and Child*, given to St. Paul's by Moore in 1984, stands near the entrance to the ambulatory.

Many of the most interesting tombs, including Wren's, are in the crypt. The most splendid is probably that of the Duke of Wellington, the Iron Duke, victor of the Battle of Waterloo in 1815. As contemporary accounts relate, his funeral here in 1852 was among the most magnificently staged events in the building's long history, rivaled for pomp and ceremony only by Winston Churchill's funeral in 1965. Also buried in the crypt are two other celebrated British military leaders: Nelson, who was killed at the battle of Trafalgar in 1805, and Kitchener, World War I military supremo, who died when the cruiser he was traveling in was struck by a mine off the Orkneys in 1916. The crypt also contains an exhibition of gold and silver plate, and ecclesiastical robes. *Tel. 071/248–2705. Admission to cathedral, ambulatory (American Chapel), crypt, and treasury £2.50 adults, £1.50 children; to galleries £2.50 adults, £1.50 children; guided 1–1½ hr. tours of the cathedral weekdays at 11, 11:30, 2, and 2:30, £3 adults, £1 children. Cathedral open for sightseeing Mon.– Sat. 8:30–4:30 (closed occasionally for special services; only limited sightseeing Sun.); ambulatory, crypt, and galleries open Mon.–Sat. 9:30–4:15, closed Sun.*

The areas immediately around St. Paul's, many of which were flattened during World War II, present a depressing contrast to the cathedral itself, despite—or perhaps because of—the earnest attempts of architects and planners after the war to make them a fitting showcase for modern British architecture. There are plans to redevelop the worst offender, Paternoster Square, but these won't take effect for some years.

The Museum of London and the Barbican

Heading north from St. Paul's up St. Martin's-le-Grand, you come to **London Wall,** a street so named because it follows the line of the old Roman wall, though only a few remains are still visible. Ironically, despite its proximity to some of the most venerable and ancient remains of London, London Wall itself ranks high among the ugliest postwar redevelopments in the City. A row of gaunt and poorly designed high-rises stretches the length of the street, discouraging all but the most determined visitors to search for the Roman remains.

⑫ But one modern building is worth seeking out here: the **Museum of London.** It traces the history of London, especially its social history, from the city's earliest days. Not to be missed among its imaginative displays are the statues from the Roman Temple of Mithras, the Lord Mayor's Ceremonial Coach, the diorama of the Great Fire of London, and the Cheapside Hoard of Jacobean jewelry, which was very likely buried for safekeeping during an outbreak of plague. The sections on the history of the capital in the present century include a Woolworth's counter and elevators from Selfridges; both stores were founded by Americans and had quite an impact on the day-to-day life of Londoners. *London Wall, tel. 071/600–3699. Admission: £3 adults, £1.50 children under 18 and senior citizens, £7.50 family ticket (up to 2 adults and 3 children); admission free 4:30–6. Open Tues.–Sat. 10–6, Sun. 2–6; closed Mon. and national holidays.*

Time Out **Millburn's,** the museum's restaurant, entered down stairs from the forecourt, provides acceptable light refreshments in an area of the City that doesn't offer much in the way of family eating places.

---

13 Just to the north of the Museum of London is another of the City's rebuilt regions, the **Barbican,** a vast residential and arts complex that is best known today as the London home of the Royal Shakespeare Company and the London Symphony Orchestra. It takes its name from the watchtower that stood here in the Middle Ages, just outside the city walls. Architecturally, about all that can be said for the Barbican is that the arts center has the largest flat roof in Europe. The residential sectors are regimented and characterless. Many residents use their apartment here as a London *pied-à-terre*, escaping to their country homes on weekends and holidays; those who live here year-round often comment on the lack of any sense of community. Furthermore, the area's gloomy concrete walkways and empty echoing plazas are no place to linger at night.

There is more life in the Barbican Arts Centre, even if it does have the feel of an air terminal run by well-heeled troglodytes. Only three of the eight levels are actually below ground, but as there are very few windows the whole place has a subterranean atmosphere. The hammered concrete walls, soft carpets, and massive girders (used decoratively as well as structurally) combine with strangely low ceilings to give one the feeling of being in an underground city. The only airy space in the whole building is the huge conservatory on the roof, open to the public only on weekends and bank holidays. Guided tours of the center take place regularly, and are a good way of seeing something of life behind the scenes.

If you can adjust to this curious atmosphere, the facilities here are unrivaled. The performances in the Royal Shakespeare Company's two auditoriums are usually well worth a visit; the main house stages a wide variety of productions in one of the most imaginatively designed auditoriums in the world. The little Pit, buried in the bowels of the building, is a small theater-in-the-round for experimental work.

Concerts take place in the Barbican Hall almost
every evening. Symphony concerts predomi-
nate, but the programs range over a very wide
spectrum. Less conventional music can be heard
in the regular program of intriguing and lively
"foyer events," which has something for almost
every taste. The Barbican Cinema shows a mixture of quality new-release films and revivals,
and the Art Gallery stages large-scale temporary exhibitions on a variety of themes. Small
art exhibitions, often displaying the creations of
just a couple of artists or craftspeople, are
mounted in the Sculpture Court and in small exhibition spaces dotted around the building. *Silk
St., tel. 071/638–4141. Admission free. Open
Mon.–Sat. 9 AM–11 PM, Sun. 12 AM–11 PM. For
theater, concert, and cinema bookings, tel. 071/
638–8891 or 071/628–2295 (recorded information). Box office open daily 10–8. Prices vary.
Barbican Gallery, tel. 071/638–4141, advance
booking tel. 071/413–3310. Prices vary according to exhibition. Open Mon.–Sat. 10–6:45,
Sun. and national holidays noon–5:45. For advance booking for tours of the center (minimum
10 people), tel. 071/628–0183. Price: £2 adults,
£1.50 children and senior citizens. For information on RSC backstage tours tel. 071/628–3351.*

Time Out   Each of the restaurants in the Barbican caters
to different tastes, and to different purses as
well. **The Cut Above** serves full-scale meals,
while the **Waterside Café,** situated next to the
terrace and pool, is the place to go for a light
meal, afternoon tea, or morning coffee. There
are also a number of bars and coffee bars in the
center.

One of the only buildings in this part of London
that survived the Blitz, and then only partially,
❶❹ is the evocatively named **St. Giles without
Cripplegate,** St. Giles being the patron saint of
cripples. Today it is the parish church of the
Barbican, and stands beside the main complex,
looking somewhat forlorn among the surrounding concrete and brick. Only the church tower
and walls are original, the remainder having
been destroyed by German bombs and rebuilt in
the 1950s.

The Guildhall and the Financial Center

Return to London Wall and head south down Coleman Street to Basinghall Avenue. Here, turn right, continue to Basinghall Street, and **⑮** you come to the **Guildhall.** This is the home of the Corporation of London, the City's governing body, presided over by the Lord Mayor of London. The building itself originally dates from about 1410, but in the course of a long and eventful life has probably sustained more damage and destruction and undergone more restoration, renovation, and outright rebuilding than any other historic building in London. It was severely damaged in the Great Fire of 1666, only the exterior stone walls surviving intact. Having been rebuilt after the fire, it underwent numerous alterations throughout the 18th and 19th centuries. Then, in 1940, it was again nearly destroyed when German bombs blew the roof off. Lavish restoration in the '50s and later again in the '70s produced the building you see today. It is the scene of the election of the Lord Mayor every year and of other City officers, and is where the City stages banquets in honor of visiting heads of state and various other bigwigs, with carriages, liveried flunkies, gold plate, and a lot of pomp and circumstance.

Visitors can see the 152-foot-long hall with its magnificent stone-arched roof. The roof itself was constructed in the 1950s, but sits upon walls dating from the Middle Ages; steel trusses hidden within the stone arches carry the weight of the roof. High up in the west gallery, well placed to observe all the ceremony below, stand Gog and Magog, 9-foot-high wooden giants. The present statues replaced two from the early 1700s that were destroyed in World War II. Gog and Magog have presided over the Guildhall since the early 1400s; Gog represents an inhabitant of ancient Britain, while Magog is a Trojan invader. *Gresham St., tel. 071/606–3030. Admission free. Open weekdays 9–5; closed national holidays.*

The new west wing of the Guildhall, built in the 1970s, houses the **Guildhall Library**—full of books and documents relating to the history of the City—and the small **Museum of the Worship-**

ful Company of Clockmakers, which contains watches and clocks from several centuries. *Tel. 071/606–3030. Admission free. Open weekdays 9:30–5; closed national holidays.*

From the Guildhall continue south down Milk Street to **Cheapside.** Memories of Saxon times haunt the streets here. The very name *Cheapside* is of Saxon origin, *ceap* meaning barter. All around Cheapside the street names—Bread Street, Ironmonger Lane, Wood Street—indicate the busy trades that flourished here from the 11th century onward. Here you will also find the church of **St. Mary-le-Bow.** There's been a church on this site since at least 1091 (contemporary records relate that its roof blew away in a gale that year), but the present building is the work of Wren. Like so many of the City's churches, it was badly damaged in the war. Tradition has it that to be a true Cockney, you must be born within the sound of Bow bells. With such a tiny permanent population in the City now, the numbers of bona-fide Cockneys have certainly been reduced.

Time Out **The Place Below,** in St. Mary-le-Bow's crypt, is a cheerful café serving breakfast and delicious vegetarian lunches on weekdays. There's a posh set meal on Thursday evenings, too.

Continue east down Cheapside and you come to the seven-way intersection that marks the center of the City. Here, the large almost windowless classical building on your left is the **Bank of England,** "the old lady of Threadneedle Street," as it has been popularly known for well over a century. The present building, which incorporates a very few parts of the original 18th-century bank, was completed just before World War II. The bank plays a leading role in Britain's economic fortunes, as well as monitoring and, when necessary, directing the multifarious goings-on of the City. It was a privately owned operation until 1946, when it was nationalized.

The **Bank of England Museum** offers exhibits and a "state-of-the-art interactive video" on the bank dealing room. *Bartholomew La., tel. 071/ 601–5545. Admission free. Open Good Friday– Sept., Mon.–Sat. and national holidays 10–6,*

Sun. 2–6; Oct.–Thurs. before Good Friday, weekdays 10–6; closed Dec. 24–26, Jan. 1.

Just behind the bank, in the narrow street called Lothbury, is the little church of **St. Margaret Lothbury.** The church was rebuilt by Wren after the Great Fire but is interesting mainly for the collection of decorative woodwork—rood screens, pews, a reredos—from a number of other Wren churches since demolished. Much of the finest work is by Grinling Gibbons.

Facing the bank, and occupying the southern flank of the intersection, is the **Mansion House,** built in the early 18th century. This is the official residence of the Lord Mayor of London. His term of office lasts just one year, and the lavish entertainments he is expected to provide are so costly that few could afford to hold the office longer. The building is not open to the public.

At the northern end of the intersection, standing at right angles to the Bank of England, is the handsome classical facade of the **Royal Exchange.** Like so much else, the first exchange was destroyed in the Great Fire of 1666. The replacement, designed along similar lines and completed in 1669 (and one of the first City buildings to be re-erected), was itself burnt down in 1838. Queen Victoria opened the present exchange in 1844, when it acquired its royal title; once again, the pattern of a central courtyard, now roofed over (and open to the public since 1992), was retained. After Lloyd's (*see below*), which had occupied space in the exchange since the 1770s, moved out to its own headquarters in 1927, the exchange experienced several decades of neglect, and was used for everything from an exhibition space for paintings by City workers to offices for an insurance company.

In 1981, the exchange reverted to something very close to its original role, becoming the home of the **London International Financial Futures Exchange.** LIFFE, as it is popularly known, enables businesses to hedge their risks in the currently volatile European market; the older Financial Futures Exchange in Chicago covers the North American market. Even if you don't understand the arcane complications of financial dealing, a trip to the Visitors' Gallery is worthwhile. Watching the trading on the floor below is like attending a performance by a combined modern dance troupe and roaring baseball crowd. *Royal Exchange, tel. 071/623–0444. Admission free. Visitors' Gallery open weekdays 11:30–1:45 (by appointment to groups of 10 or more from relevant organizations); closed national holidays.*

Time Out If you want to mingle with the stressed-out buyers and sellers on a break from the exchange floor, join them at the **Greenhouse Steak Bar** (expensive snacks are also served) at the back of the Royal Exchange. Or go to Finch Lane for a couple of pints at the **Woolpack,** a basic, smoky pub, with not much more food than a cheese or ham roll, but plenty of opportunity for eavesdropping.

The raison d'être of the City has always been to trade and to make money, and LIFFE is but one of the latest and most successful manifestations of that purpose. If you head down Threadneedle Street between the Bank of England and the Royal Exchange, you will reach a much more ㉑ venerable trading institution, the **London Stock Exchange.** There has been a stock exchange in London since at least the beginning of the 18th century. It moved from one location to another as it grew, settling here in 1801. The present building, opened in 1972, is the third on this site. Trading in stocks and shares used to take place on the trading floor, which often became hectic and confused. Following the so-called "Big Bang" in the fall of 1986, when computerization and a number of reforms of stock exchange trading practices were implemented, trading has moved off the floor. Business is now done almost exclusively over the telephone; the offices of all the stock exchange member companies are linked by a sophisticated electronic network that gives up-to-the-minute information on the share prices of some 7,000 companies all over the world. As a result, a visit to the Viewing Gallery is likely to be disappointing, as only one corner of the trading floor is now regularly used; this is for the Traded Options Market. Short talks are given on the workings of the stock exchange (now the largest exchange in the world, executing, on average, 30,000 orders each working day), and there are regular films, but modern technology has left the gallery behind, and it doesn't have much atmosphere. *Old Broad St., tel. 071/588–2355. Admission free. Open weekdays 9:30–5:30; closed national holidays.*

Another of London's great financial institutions, **Lloyd's,** has its headquarters here in Leadenhall Street. To reach it from the stock exchange, turn right into Gracechurch Street and then take the first left into Leadenhall Street. This route takes you near **Leadenhall Market,** where there has been a market since the 14th century. The present building, all glass and brightly painted cast iron, dates from 1881.

㉒ Lloyd's of London has been in the insurance business since the end of the 17th century. But as if to belie its long and distinguished history, the firm's new headquarters are anything but traditional. Finished in 1986, they are the work of the modernist architect Richard Rogers, whose other well-known buildings include the Pompidou Center in Paris.

The building, which cost £163 million, has been the target of much criticism, but it undoubtedly is the most lively and imaginative of all the new blocks in the City, with far more visual interest than, say, the monolithic National Westminster Bank Tower a short distance to the north. The main feature of Lloyd's is a 200-foot-high barrel vault made of sparkling glass specially treated to make it appear "alive" from wherever you see it, inside or out, and in all weather. The barrel vault houses a central atrium, or court, around which are wrapped 12 tiers of galleries stretching toward the sky. From inside, you feel as if you're in a majestic medieval cathedral, with light streaming in through the great glass window. Almost as striking are the six satellite towers, all metal and exposed pipes, which accommodate the building's heating plant and other maintenance services.

A public visit to Lloyd's must be arranged at least a week in advance by application in writing on headed paper from a "recognized organization." The visit starts with a ride in one of the many external glass-sided observation elevators, another novel (for London) feature of the building. Then you visit an exhibition that tells the history of Lloyd's from its origins at the end of the 17th century in Edward Lloyd's coffee house on nearby Tower Street, where insurance was arranged for trading ships and their cargoes. The culmination of the visit is the view from one of the galleries down into the great atrium and lower galleries.

There is also an exhibition illustrating the history of Lloyd's. The Lutine Bell, traditionally rung to announce the loss at sea of a vessel insured with Lloyd's, now stands in the center of the atrium and is only rung occasionally—two strokes for good news, one for bad. *1 Lime St., tel. 071/623–7100, ext. 6210 or 5786. Open weekdays 10–2:30 to groups of 10 or more by appointment; closed national holidays.*

Time Out **Lloyd's Coffee House,** at the foot of the new office building, serves virtually anything throughout the day: breakfast, a full lunch, afternoon tea, or just coffee and pastries. Despite its name, there's no connection, even in terms of decor, with the 17th-century coffee house where Lloyd's originated.

Mithras, the Monument, and London Bridge

Most of our route so far has been over the area once occupied by the Roman settlement. During the last 40 years or so, archaeologists have been able to piece together a fairly comprehensive picture of the Roman city; another piece was fitted into the jigsaw early in 1988 when the remains of an amphitheater were discovered on a construction site in front of the Guildhall. It is hoped that these newly discovered remains, part of one of the most important buildings of Roman Londinium, will eventually be incorporated into some form of permanent exhibition. Naturally enough, there is scarcely any visible evidence of the period of Roman occupation on the present-day streets; some of the archaeological finds are on display in the Museum of London, from which you can also view a section of the Roman city walls. However, if you retrace your steps to the Bank of England and then head southwest down Queen Victoria Street for a few **(23)** hundred yards, you'll reach the **Temple of Mithras,** unearthed during construction work in 1954. Further Roman remains are on show in Cannon Street, just around the corner. Here is the **London Stone** set, oddly enough, into the wall of the Bank of China. Though its origins are unknown, it is believed that this is the ancient Roman milestone from which all distances throughout the province of Britannia were measured.

Continue down Cannon Street and into Eastcheap. From here turn right into Fish Street **(24)** Hill. Before you is the **Monument,** a massive Doric column of white stone put up in 1667—and designed, naturally enough, by Wren—to commemorate the Great Fire of London, ". . . the better to preserve the memory of this dreadful Visitation," as the Act of Parliament that allowed for its construction put it. The Monument stands 202 feet high, with its base exactly 202 feet from the small bakery shop in Pudding Lane where the fire started. At the summit is a gilt urn with flames leaping from it. You can climb up to the top (311 steps) and admire the fine view. St. Paul's looms close by, though now it has to compete with modern tower blocks. *Monument St., tel. 071/626–2717. Admission: £1 adults, 25p children. Open Mon.–Sat. 9–2.*

(25) A little to the south of the Monument is **London Bridge.** A bridge has been at or near the site of the present London Bridge since Roman times, although the exact location of the earliest bridge is unknown. Recent research suggests that it was probably a little downstream from today's bridge. A second wooden bridge certainly existed in Saxon times, and this is the one that seems to have given rise to the nursery rhyme *London Bridge is Falling Down,* which it really did in 1014. The first stone bridge was constructed in 1176. It rapidly sprouted houses along both sides of its narrow width and stood until 1831, when it was finally pulled down to make way for an elegant, classical structure. The opening ceremony took the form of a banquet on the bridge itself, to which 15,000 people were invited. This bridge was in turn replaced in 1967 when it could no longer cope with the volume of traffic, and was sold to the McCulloch Oil Corporation of California, which reconstructed it at Lake Havasu City, in a corner of America's Arizona desert; rumor has it the company mistakenly thought that they were buying the infinitely more spectacular Tower Bridge. The present London Bridge is more than 100 feet wide and divides the Port of London, downstream, from King's Reach, upstream.

From London Bridge head down Lower Thames Street to what was, until 1982, **Billingsgate Fish Market.** Beside the old market building, now hardly recognizable as it has undergone a thorough reconstruction, is the Custom House, built early in the last century. Just to the east of here, back in Lower Thames Street, substantial remains of a wooden Roman jetty were unearthed a few years ago. The bulk of the finds are now in the Museum of London.

The Tower of London

From Lower Thames Street it's an easy five-minute walk to the most famous of the City's sights, the **Tower of London.** Of all the historic monuments and buildings of London, the Tower of London (or simply the Tower, as it is generally known) is perhaps the most impressive and rewarding to visit—a dramatic and beautiful series of buildings intimately bound to the story of London.

The Tower began life as a fortress and palace, and it remains one of the Royal Palaces (in which capacity it guards the Crown Jewels). The Queen does not live here, of course, though every British monarch from William the Conqueror in the 11th century to Henry VIII in the 16th did. At other times the Tower has been the site of the Royal Mint; home to the Public Records, the Royal Menagerie, and the Royal Observatory; and, most famously, a prison and scene of countless executions. Those who were incarcerated here included Anne Boleyn; Queen Elizabeth I, before she came to the throne; Sir Walter Raleigh, who spent 13 years here; and Robert Devereux, Earl of Essex and long-time favorite

of Elizabeth I. The little Princes in the Tower
may also have also met their fates here.

Its splendor and its richly historic associations
make the Tower a hugely popular tourist attraction. It gets *very* crowded, especially in the
summer. So be prepared for long lines, and allow at least three hours for a visit. A good time
to arrive is early in the morning, when the Tower opens. If you visit before April 1994, head
straight for the Crown Jewels, and you should
be able to see them in relative peace before the
crowds build up. (Remember that the Jewel
House is normally closed throughout Febru-
ary.) In April, the jewels move to the ground
floor of the **Duke of Wellington's Barracks.** Their
new home will, after its £10 million renovation,
accommodate four times the visitor volume of
the old Jewel House—thanks partly to a section
of moving floor that will ensure you don't drool
too long over the most important jewels.

The best and most interesting way to see the
buildings, at any rate on a first visit, is to tag
along on one of the many free tours given by the
"Beefeaters," the popular name for the Yeoman
Warders of the Tower. They wear a distinctive
and picturesque Tudor-style uniform of dark
blue and red and, on special occasions, an even
more magnificent one of scarlet and gold. Tours
start from the Middle Tower about every 30 minutes; they last approximately one hour, and the
Warders' commentary is full of factual detail.

The Tower straddles almost exactly the line of
the old Roman city walls of London, fragments
of which can be seen at the little **Wardrobe Tower**
at the southeast corner of the **White Tower**—the
heart of the entire complex, and in some ways
the most impressive, certainly the most conspic-
uous, building here. It is also the oldest, begun
in 1078 by William the Conqueror, the first Norman king of England, and completed in about
1097. The interior has been greatly altered—
except for the **Chapel of St. John,** which is the
original Norman chapel, as beautiful as it is
rare. It is a structure of great simplicity, almost
entirely lacking in ornamentation, built in char-
acteristically heavy Norman style. It is one of

the great treasures of London and should not be missed.

The rest of the White Tower is occupied by the **Royal Armouries,** Britain's national museum of arms and armor. The armor and weapons on display come from both Britain and the rest of Europe, and date from Saxon and Viking times up to the present day. Among the highlights are four personal armors of Henry VIII, one with matching horse armor; the armors of several of Elizabeth's favorites, including Robert Dudley, Earl of Leicester; and the gilt armor of Charles I. The Tower's instruments of torture and punishment, including the block and axe, are displayed in the basement of the White Tower. In the **New Armouries** there are examples of almost every weapon made for the British soldier from the 17th to the 19th century.

Surrounding the White Tower are other fortifications and buildings, dating from the 11th to the 19th century. Starting from the main entrance (by the shop), the first and most obvious feature is the **moat.** Until it was drained under the direction of the Duke of Wellington in 1843, the moat was foully polluted, obstinately resisting all attempts to flush it with water from the Thames. When the Tower's ravens die, they are buried in a graveyard for them in a section of drained moat.

Across the moat a series of gateways—the **Middle Tower** and the **Byward Tower**—form the principal entrance on this, the landward approach. A little farther on the right you will reach **Traitors' Gate,** which used to be the river entrance. Its name comes from the time when it was the main entrance to the Tower, for the Thames acted as London's chief thoroughfare, and condemned prisoners, or those under suspicion, were delivered by water to their grim fate.

Immediately opposite Traitors' Gate is the misleadingly named **Bloody Tower.** Begun as a water gate in about 1220, it was originally known as the Garden Tower, and its present name can be traced back only as far as 1571. Its most famous inmates were the little Princes in the Tower—Edward V and his younger brother—incarcerated here in 1483 on the orders of their uncle, who then claimed the throne as Richard III after they disappeared, presumably murdered. There is no clear proof of Richard's guilt, but there is little reason to doubt that they did die either here or somewhere else in the Tower. Sir Walter Raleigh was also a prisoner here between 1603 and 1616, and spent his time writing a *History of the World.*

Next to the Bloody Tower is the **Wakefield Tower,** a ponderous circular structure built in the 13th century. Originally it contained the king's private apartments. Henry VI was allegedly murdered here in 1471, another of the many victims of the Wars of the Roses, England's bloody medieval civil war.

Beyond Wakefield Tower and inside the inner wall, or ward, you are faced by the great bulk of the **White Tower.** The first things you might notice are the ravens, long a feature of the Tower. The ravens' wings are clipped to be sure they don't leave; legend has it that the disappearance of the ravens will signal the disintegration of the kingdom. Though picturesque, the birds are not exactly friendly; they have been known to attack visitors, so be on your guard.

Running the length of the inner ward on the east side is a series of buildings dating from the 17th, 18th, and 19th centuries. These are the **New Armouries,** the **Old Hospital,** and the **Museum of the Royal Fusiliers.**

By far the most famous exhibit here—for many people the principal attraction in the whole Tower—is the Crown Jewels, a priceless and breathtakingly beautiful collection of regalia, precious stones, gold, and silver, all housed in the high-security buildings known as the **Jewel House** until April 1994, and after that in the **Duke of Wellington's Barracks** (*see above*). Perhaps the most startling exhibits are the Royal Scepter, containing the largest cut diamond in the world, weighing in at no less than 530 carats, and the Imperial State Crown, made for the coronation of Queen Victoria in 1838 and containing some 3,000 precious stones, including the second-largest cut diamond in the world. Like that in the Royal Scepter, it was cut from the Cullinan diamond—the Star of Africa. Almost as extraordinary is the immense Kohinoor diamond, set in the crown made for the coronation of George VI's queen, Elizabeth (now the Queen Mother), in 1937.

The little chapel of **St. Peter ad Vincula** can be visited only as part of a Yeoman Warder tour. St. Peter ad Vincula is the resting place of the many people executed at the Tower; Anne Boleyn and Catherine Howard are known to be buried here (under the altar). A plaque on the rear wall details many of the more celebrated. Being "traitors," however, they were not accorded normal burial, and their corpses were simply dumped under the flagstones. In all, some 2,000 bodies are thought to have been buried here (all the bones were reburied in the walls during Victorian renovations).

Directly outside the chapel is **Tower Green,** which was used both as an overflow burial ground when it eventually became impossible to accommodate more corpses in the chapel, and as the site of the very small number of private executions that were carried out at the Tower. A small bronze tablet marks the spot where the block is believed to have been positioned. It was a rare honor to be granted the privilege of a private execution on Tower Green. Most people were unceremoniously executed outside the Tower on nearby Tower Hill: Apart from anything else, it afforded a much better view for the thousands who regularly flocked to the executions.

To the west of Tower Green is the **Beauchamp Tower,** built by Edward I (who reigned 1272–1307). The walls are liberally strewn with graffiti and inscriptions carved by prisoners. Many are in Latin, but there are also names—including one that has traditionally been assumed to refer to Lady Jane Grey, England's "nine-day Queen," imprisoned in the Tower and executed for high treason in 1554, at the age of 16.

Immediately to the south of the Beauchamp Tower is an *L*-shape row of black-and-white Tudor houses. The center one is known as the **Queen's House,** and was built in 1530 for the governor of the Tower. By tradition, Anne Boleyn was imprisoned here before her execution, and it was here that the conspirators of the 1605 Gunpowder Plot to blow up Parliament were interrogated. Queen's House also detained the Tower's last prisoner—Rudolph Hess, the Nazi who parachuted into London in 1941 to seek asylum.

An excellent overview of the Tower can now be had from the battlements. A walk along the walls of the inner ward, beginning at the **Wakefield Tower** and taking in many of the defensive towers, provides a fitting climax to a visit to the Tower of London. *HM Tower of London, tel. 071/709–0765. Admission: £6.70 adults, £4.40 children under 15, £5.10 senior citizens, £19 family (2 adults, 3 children); reduced admission charges apply during Jan., when the Jewel House is closed. Small additional admission charge to the Fusiliers Museum only. Open Mar.–Oct., Mon.–Sat. 9:30–5, Sun. 2–5; Nov.–Feb., Mon.–Sat. 9:30–4; closed Good Friday, Dec. 24–26, Jan. 1. For tickets to Ceremony of the Keys (the locking of the main gates, nightly at 10 PM), write well in advance from your home address to The Resident Governor and Keeper of the Jewel House, Queen's House, HM Tower of London, EC3. Give your name, dates you wish to attend (including alternate dates), and number of people (up to 7), and enclose a stamped, addressed envelope.*

Yeoman Warder guides daily from Middle Tower, no charge, but a tip is always appreciated. Subject to weather and availability of guides, about every 30 min until 3:30 in summer, 2:30 in winter.

From the riverside walk in front of the Tower; **28** there is a good view across to **H.M.S. *Belfast*** and the new building developments along the south bank of the Thames.

To the west of the Tower is a new development, where various shops and food outlets surround **29** the entrance to **Tower Hill Pageant,** London's first dark-ride museum. Automated cars take visitors past mock-ups of scenes from the past, complete with "people," sound effects, and smells. There's also an archaeological museum with finds from the Thames. *Tower Hill Terrace, tel. 071/709–0081. Admission: £4.50 adults,*

*£2.50 children under 16 and senior citizens.
Open Apr.–Oct., daily 9:30–5:30; Nov.–Mar.,
daily 9:30–4:30; closed Dec. 25.*

Tower Bridge and St. Katharine's Dock

30 **Tower Bridge,** just to the east of the Tower of London, was begun in 1885 and opened with due pomp and ceremony nine years later by the then Prince of Wales, later Edward VII. It's unusual among London's bridges in that it is the only bridge that can be raised to allow ships to pass. Today, of course, with the virtual extinction of trade and ship movements on the Thames in London, the complex lifting mechanism is used only four or five times a week. The bridge is also one of only a handful over the Thames built in the Gothic style. This was done principally to ensure that it harmonized with the nearby Tower of London, but it is also the major reason why so many people have inadvertently assumed that the bridge actually dates from the Middle Ages, and mistake it for London Bridge.

By way of a gift for its hundredth birthday (in 1994), Tower Bridge has been given a complete overhaul, taking it way up in the worth-visiting stakes. A new permanent exhibition replaces the old, somewhat dull up-across-and-down-again visit. It starts in a similar vein, with an elevator ride up the North Tower, but then becomes an audiovisual time-traveling journey into the history, construction, and *raison d'être* of London's most distinctive bridge. The show (which wasn't yet up at press time) features "Compact Disc Interactive Technology" superimposing the skyline of ages past over today's view, various models and dramatizations of Victorian London, animatronic tour guides, and a reenactment of the Engine Room's Royal Opening. Fortunately, the walkways are still open, too. *Tel. 071/403–3761. Admission: £2.50 adults, £1 children under 15 and senior citizens. Open Apr.–Oct., daily 10–6:30; Nov.–Mar., daily 10–4:45; closed Good Friday, Dec. 24–25, Jan. 1.*

31 To the east of the Tower is **St. Katharine's Dock.** The best route from the Tower is along the wharf, underneath Tower Bridge and then along the path in front of the Tower Hotel. The Dock was opened in 1828, but was never very successful, partly because, as you can still see today, the entrance from the river was too small to accommodate large ships. The Dock closed in 1968, and after a lot of controversy the site was redeveloped; sadly, some of the handsome warehouses that once lined the dockside were demolished and replaced with a combination of modern shops, offices, flats, and a large hotel; but a few renovated warehouses do remain, and the docks themselves are used as a marina.

Other Attractions

The British Museum, one of the world's greatest museums, is a monumental, severely Greek edifice, built in the first half of the 19th century. The vast collection of treasures here includes Egyptian, Greek, and Roman antiquities; Renaissance jewelry, pottery, coins, glass; and drawings from virtually every European school since the 15th century. It's best to concentrate on one area that particularly interests you or, alternatively, take one of the museum's guided tours, which cost £6 per person and last 1½ hours. Some of the highlights are the Elgin Marbles, sculptures from the Parthenon in Athens; the Rosetta Stone, which helped archaeologists decipher Egyptian hieroglyphics; and the Mildenhall Treasure, a cache of Roman silver found in East Anglia in 1842. *Great Russell St., tel. 071/636–1555 or 071/580–1788 (recorded information). Admission free. Open Mon.–Sat. 10–5, Sun. 2:30–6.*

The Gardens of the Zoological Society of London, known simply as the Zoo, were founded over 150 years ago, absorbing over the years other collections, such as the royal menagerie, which used to be housed in the Tower of London. One fascinating exhibit is the Moonlight World, on the lower floor of the Charles Clore Pavilion. Here night conditions are simulated so that visitors can watch nocturnal animals during the day. *Regent's Park, tel. 071/722–3333. Admission: £6 adults, £4 children under 16, £5 senior citizens. Open summer, daily 9–6; winter, daily 10–4.*

Madame Tussaud's still maintains its position as one of London's most sought-after attractions, with an ever-changing parade of wax celebrities. Get there early to avoid the long lines. *Marylebone Rd., tel. 071/935–6861. Admission: £6.40 adults, £4.15 children under 16, £4.80 senior citizens. Joint ticket with Planetarium, £8.30 adults, £5.35 children, £6.40 senior citizens. Open Easter–Sept., daily 9:30–5:30; Oct.–Easter, daily 10–5:30.*

The London Planetarium, beside Madame Tussaud's, brings the night sky to life. There are also displays of holography and interactive videos. *Marylebone Rd., tel. 071/486–1121. Admission: £3.80 adults, £2.40 children under 16, £2.95 senior citizens. Joint ticket with Madame Tussaud's, see above. Shows every 40 min; weekends 10:40–5:20, weekdays 12:40–4:40; extra shows during school vacations.*

Lincoln's Inn Fields is the capital's largest and oldest square—more like a small park—surrounded by handsome buildings. The magnificent 1806 portico on the south side fronts the Royal College of Surgeons. The square's great attraction, however, is **Sir John Soane's Museum,** one of the most idiosyncratic and fascinating museums in London. Sir John Soane, who lived here from 1790 to 1831, was a gifted architect and an avid collector. The exhibits include Hogarth's series of paintings *The Rake's Progress,* and the sarcophagus of the Egyptian emperor Seti I, which Soan bought for £2,000 after the British Museum refused it. *13 Lincoln's Inn Fields, tel. 071/405–2107. Admission free. Open Tues.–Sat. 10–5; closed national holidays.*

What to See and Do with Children

On London's traditional sightseeing circuit, make for the **Royal Mews** (*see* Westminster and Royal London), where some of the Queen's horses can be seen up close, the **Changing of the Guard,** with its colorful pomp and circumstance (*see* Westminster and Royal London), the **Whispering Gallery** in **St. Paul's Cathedral** (*see* The

City), where it is fun to try the echo, and the gruesome instruments of torture on show in the **Bowyer Tower** in the **Tower of London** (*see* The City). Climb the 311 steps to the top of the **Monument** (*see* The City), or take the elevator to the high walkways of **Tower Bridge** (*see* The City). At **Hampton Court** see who can find their way out of the maze first.

Kidsline is a computerized information service with details on current events that might interest children. Call 071/222–8000 during office hours for information.

Museums of specific interest to children include the **London Transport Museum** in Covent Garden (*see* Soho and Covent Garden); the **Science Museum,** where there are lots of opportunities for hands-on discovery; the **London Toy & Model Museum** north of Kensington Gardens, which offers model railroads and rides (Sunday only) on a narrow-gauge steam track; the **Bethnal Green Museum of Childhood** in east London, which has traditional toys, dolls, dolls' houses, and puppets; and the **Horniman Museum,** an educational museum set in 16 acres of gardens in south London with well-displayed ethnographic and natural history collections and a new Music Gallery.

London Toy & Model Museum, *21–23 Craven Hill, tel. 071/262–9450. Admission: £3 adults, £1.50 children under 15, £2 senior citizens. Open Tues.–Sat. 10–5:30, Sun. 11–5:30; closed all Mons. except national holidays, Good Friday, Dec. 24–25, Jan. 1.*

Bethnal Green Museum of Childhood, *Cambridge Heath Rd., tel. 081/980–3204 or 081/980–2415. Admission free. Open Mon.–Thurs. and Sat. 10–6, Sun. 2:30–6; closed Friday, Dec. 24–26, Jan. 1.*

Horniman Museum, *100 London Rd., Forest Hill, tel. 081/699–1872/2339. Admission free. Open Mon.–Sat. 10:30–6, Sun. 2–6.*

Other attractions include **Guinness World of Records,** in the Trocadero Centre at Piccadilly Circus (*see* Soho and Covent Garden), and the London **Zoo** in Regent's Park (*see* Other Attractions, *above*).

Older children might appreciate the Madame Tussaud's offshoot, **Rock Circus,** where replicas of everyone from Elvis to Madonna go through their paces amid the odd laser and a *loud* soundtrack. At the other extreme of automated entertainment, the **Cabaret Mechanical Theatre** is a charming small exhibition of hand-built wood and metal sculptures large and small, which move when buttons are pressed or handles cranked. Some are very funny and suitable for adults.

There are two sophisticated theme parks on the very edge of the built-up area of the capital city: **Chessington World of Adventures,** to the south, where there is also a zoo, and **Thorpe Park,** toward the west.

Cabaret Mechanical Theatre, *33–34 The Market, Covent Garden Piazza, tel. 071/379–7961. Admission: £1.75 adults, £1 children and senior citizens. Open Tues.–Sun. 10–6:30, Mon. noon–6:30.*

Chessington World of Adventures, *Leatherhead Rd., Chessington, Surrey, tel. 03727/27227. Admission: £10.75 adults, £9.75 children, £5 senior citizens. Open daily 10–5. Oct.–Mar. the zoo alone is open; admission: £3 adults, £2 children 4–14 and senior citizens; under-4s free.*

Rock Circus, *London Pavilion, Piccadilly Circus, tel. 071/734–8025. Admission: £6.25 adults, £4.25 children, £5.25 senior citizens. Open Sun., Mon., Wed., Thurs. 11–9, Tues. noon–9, Fri. and Sat. 11–10. Closed Dec. 25.*

Thorpe Park, *Staines Rd., Chertsey, Surrey, tel. 0932/562633. Admission: £9.95 adults, £8.95 children under 14, £7 senior citizens. Open daily Apr.–Oct. 10–6.*

3 Shopping

Shopping Districts

Camden Town Around Camden Lock and the other weekend markets, an impressive array of complementary shops has emerged over recent years. The style will suit those of bohemian tendencies, with crafts both made by British designers and imported from sunnier continents. The area is good for cheap clothing of the T-shirts-boots-and-vintage type.

Chelsea Chelsea means first and foremost the King's Road, less glamorous now than a few years ago, and no longer a mecca for those in search of up-to-the-minute fashion. Chelsea is a happy hunting ground for the antiques lover and the discriminating home furnisher. Clothing can also be a good buy.

Covent Garden Crafts shops, clothing stores, and design-conscious retailers have made a natural home for themselves here, especially in and around the elegantly restored 19th-century market. But this is one of those delightful areas where simply strolling around, window shopping, and people watching are as much fun as the shopping itself.

Hampstead For picturesque peace and quiet with your shopping, stroll around here midweek. Upscale clothing stores and representatives of the better chains share the half dozen streets with cozy boutique-size shops for the home and stomach.

Kensington Antiques are the real draw here, especially up Kensington Church Street, but you'd better be serious—the prices certainly will be. Kensington High Street itself is a smaller, less crowded version of Oxford Street, with some good-quality mid-price clothing shops and larger stores at the east end.

Knightsbridge This is very much a home-away-from-home for the committed shopper. Heading the list is Harrods, its great gaudy Edwardian bulk dominating Brompton Road. But there are delights all around. Sloane Street—for fashions and fabrics, with the modish Harvey Nichols at the Knightsbridge end—Beauchamp Place, neighboring Walton Street, and Brompton Cross, at the start of Fulham Road, all boast the sort of tempting one-of-a-kind fashion and design emporia that defy you not to part with money.

Mayfair Mayfair means Bond Street (Old and New), South Molton Street, Savile Row, and the Burlington Arcade, in an area lying between Piccadilly and Oxford Street. The emphasis is very much on traditional British goods and international brand names, with South Molton Street adding a raffish, modern accent. Prices and quality are tiptop.

Oxford Street Despite its claim to be Britain's premier shopping street, Oxford Street is to be endured rather than enjoyed. Selfridges, Marks and Spencer, and John Lewis are all good department stores here, while little St. Christopher's Place and Gees Court, almost opposite the Bond Street tube, add a chic touch. But otherwise the crowds, the noise, the traffic, and the unmistakable tattiness of stretches of Oxford Street itself combine to produce a very much less-than-lovely atmosphere.

Piccadilly Though the actual number of shops here is really quite low for a street of its length—after all, Green Park takes up almost half of one side— Piccadilly still boasts a number of classy outfits, Simpsons, Hatchards, and Fortnum and Mason chief among them. Also in the Piccadilly area are several very elegant shopping arcades, with the Burlington Arcade leading the pack.

Regent Street China, clothes, fabrics, good department stores, and wide sidewalks have all helped make Regent Street an appealing alternative to neighboring Oxford Street. The crowds are just as thick on the ground, but the presence of perennials such as Liberty—probably the city's most appealing department store—more than compensate.

Specialty Stores

Antiques **Antiquarius** (131–141 King's Rd., SW3) at the Sloane Square end of the King's Road is an indoor antiques market with over 200 stalls that offers a wide variety of collectibles, including metalware, meerschaum pipes, ceramics, and art nouveau bric-à-brac.

Gray's Antique Market (58 Davies St., W1) and around the corner **Gray's Mews** (1–7 Davies Mews, W1) are a vast gaggle of small boutiques loaded with curios and collectibles. This is a hunting ground for the keen searcher for treasure trove—but allow yourself plenty of time.

China and Glass **Gered** (158 Regent St., W1) is the store to go to for that wedding gift. It has a huge selection of designs to choose from, with a heavy emphasis on Wedgwood, many of whose most popular designs date back to the 18th century. There are also branches at 112 Regent Street, W1, and 173 Piccadilly, W1.

Clothing To shop at **Burberrys** (161–165 Regent St., W1, and 18–22 The Haymarket, SW1) is rather like visiting a comfortably familiar country house, where closets and drawers spill over with classic, quality clothing for men and women. Famous for its tartan trademark and its magnificent raincoats.

Kensington Market (49–53 Kensington High St., W8) is the diametric opposite of sober British stiff-upper-lip anti-fashion. For over two decades it has been a principal purveyor of the constantly changing, frivolous, hip London street style. Hundreds of stalls—some shop-size, others tiny—are crammed into this building, where you can get lost for hours trying to find the good bits.

Marks & Spencer (458 Oxford St., W1, and 173 Oxford St., W1). This major chain of stores is an integral part of the British way of life—sturdy practical clothes, good materials and workmanship, and basic accessories, all at moderate, though not bargain basement, prices. "Marks and Sparks," as they are popularly known, have never been renowned for their high style, though that is changing as they continue to bring in (anonymously) big-name designers to spice up their lines. There are two major branches on Oxford Street, #458 near Marble Arch and the other, #173, just east of Oxford Circus.

Simpson (203 Piccadilly, W1) is a quiet, pleasant store, with a thoughtful variety of designer and leisure wear, luggage, and gifts. It is the home

Shopping A (Mayfair, Soho, and Covent Garden)

The Armoury of
St. James's, **19**
Asprey's, **17**
Browns, **4**
Burberrys, **14, 21**
Butler and
Wilson, **5**
Contemporary
Applied Arts, **27**
Craftsmen
Potters Shop, **11**
Garrard, **15**

Gered, **13**
Gray's Antique
Market, **6**
Grosvenor
Prints, **26**
Halcyon Days, **7**
Hamleys, **12**
The Irish Linen
Co., **18**
Liberty, **9**
Marks &
Spencer, **1, 10**
Moss Bros., **16, 23**

Naturally
British, **22**
Nicole Farhi, **3**
Ray Man, **29**
Rebecca, **24**
Sam Walker, **28**
Selfridges, **2**
Simpson, **20**
The Tea
House, **25**
Warehouse, **8**

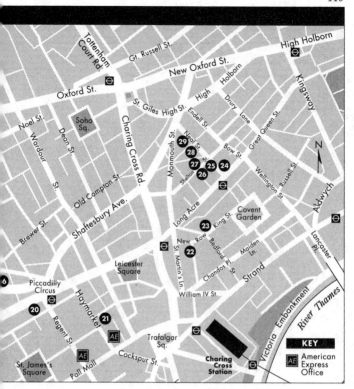

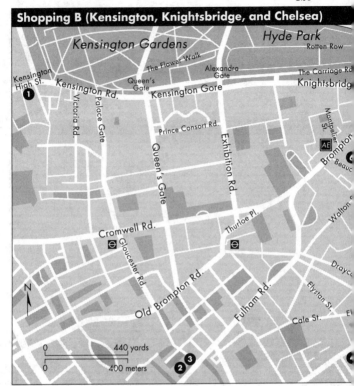

Antiquarius, **4**

Browns, **9**

Butler and
Wilson, **3**

General Trading
Co., **5**

Harrods, **7**

Janet Reger, **6**

Kensington
Market, **1**

Theo Fennel, **2**

Warehouse, **8**

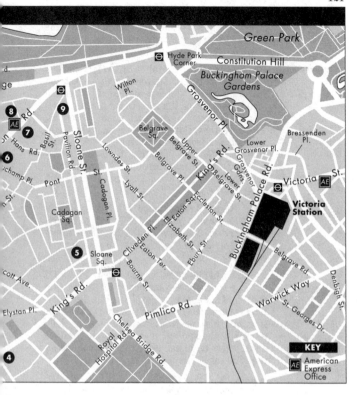

Green Park

Hyde Park Corner

Constitution Hill

Buckingham Palace Gardens

Wilton Pl.

Grosvenor Pl.

Belgrave Sq.

Lower Grosvenor Pl.

Bressenden Pl.

Sloane St.

Pavilion Rd.

Basil St.

Hans Rd.

Beauchamp Pl.

Pont St.

Lowndes St.

Lyall St.

Belgrave Pl.

Upper Belgrave St.

King's Rd.

Grosvenor Gdns.

Lower Belgrave St.

Victoria St.

Cadogan Sq.

St. Cadogan Pl.

Cliveden Pl.

Eaton Sq.

Eaton Ter.

Eccleston St.

Elizabeth St.

Ebury St.

Buckingham Palace Rd.

Victoria Station

Belgrave Rd.

Sloane Sq.

Bourne St.

Denbigh St.

Prescott Ave.

Elystan Pl.

King's Rd.

Chelsea Bridge Rd.

Royal Hospital Rd.

Pimlico Rd.

Warwick Way

St. Georges Dr.

KEY

AE American Express Office

of the Daks' brand of classic British design. There are a barbershop, restaurant, and wine bar to add to the store's conveniences. It's just a block west of Piccadilly Circus.

Women's Wear **Browns** (23–27 South Molton St., W1) is the firm that put the South Molton Street pedestrian mall on the map, and is a very good bet for the trendy shopper on the lookout for the latest designer clothes. Here you'll find styles by Azzedine Alaïa, Donna Karan, Romeo Gigli, and all the latest from France, Italy, Germany, the United States and, of course, Britain. The Labels for Less section offers up to 70% reductions on end-of-lines and seconds. Also at 6C Sloane Street, SW1.

Janet Reger (2 Beauchamp Pl., SW3). It was Janet Reger who pioneered the surge of luxurious lingerie that now froths out from every store. This is the one, though, to visit for the real thing.

Nicole Farhi (25–26 St. Christopher's Pl., W1). A store specially recommended for the career woman of taste, Nicole Farhi stocks a desirable range of practical clothes. Prices are on the high side, but there is some affordable wear as well, especially the sporty, casual Diversion range. Farhi offers an equally desirable men's line as well. Also at 27 Hampstead High Street, NW3.

Warehouse (19 Argyll St., W1). Warehouse stocks practical, stylish, reasonably priced separates, in easy fabrics and lots of fun colors. The finishing isn't so hot, but style, not substance, counts here, and the shop's youthful fans don't seem to mind. The stock changes very quickly, so it always presents a new face to the world. Also at 76 Brompton Road, SW3, as well as other locations.

Men's Wear **Moss Bros.** (27 King St., WC2, and 88 Regent St., W1). "Moss Bross," as you will always hear this store called, made their name renting out tuxedos, complete morning suits for fancy weddings, and all kinds of formal wear for the busy man—and woman—on the move. The store on King Street will save you having to pack your tux just in case of that formal date. The Regent Street store stocks an excellent range of menswear for sale, both formal and leisure, mostly in a middle range of prices.

Sam Walker (41 Neal St., WC2) provides a refined way to buy secondhand clothes. He specializes in men's vintage clothing at prices that *almost* reflect their near-museum quality. Naturally, most of the stock is well pre-World War II, and carries period nostalgia in every fold. There's also a women's version, called **Rebecca,** at #66.

Crafts Some of the best British potters joined to found the **Craftsmen Potters Shop** (7 Marshall St., W1) as a cooperative venture to market their wares. The result is a store that carries a wide spectrum of the potter's art, from thoroughly practical pitchers, plates, and bowls to ceramic sculptures. Prices range from the reasonable to way up.

Craftworks (31 Southend Rd., NW3; tube stop: Hampstead) is a haven packed with handmade table- and glassware, ceramics, candlesticks, wall hangings, and mirrors from all over the world—and also from just down the road.

At **Contemporary Applied Arts** (43 Earlham St., WC2), a mixed bag of designers and craftspeople display their wares over two floors. Anything from glassware and jewelry to furniture and lighting can be found here.

True to its name, **Naturally British** (13 New Row, WC2) is a good spot to find British crafts, from small, low-priced pottery or wood items to larger pieces, such as gloriously carved rocking horses with high price tags on their aristocratic manes.

Gifts **The Armoury of St. James's** (17 Piccadilly Arcade, SW1). The Armoury is a fascinating wee store bursting with impeccably painted toy soldiers, old medals, and military prints. A must for the nostalgia enthusiast.

General Trading Co. (144 Sloane St., SW1). With a dozen departments to explore, even the most finicky shopper will find something to delight or amuse in this Aladdin's cave. General Trading Company buyers range the world—especially the Far East—to discover new suppliers, and their merchandise includes French glass, Indian crafts, Italian lighting fixtures, Chinese toys, and English bone china. This is one of those delightfully absorbing shops where you can spend as little as £5, or as much as your credit card will stretch to, and you will always feel you are walking away with something special.

Halcyon Days (14 Brook St., W1) is a charming shop devoted entirely to small decorative boxes—from music boxes to snuffboxes—made of enamel, china, or precious metals. They have a very decorative line in commemorative items, which make ideal mementos.

Hamleys (188–196 Regent St., W1). Six floors of toys and games for both children and adults. The huge stock ranges from traditional teddy bears to computer games and all the latest technological gimmickry. Try to avoid it at Christmas, when police have to rope off a section of Regent Street for Hamleys customers.

Ray Man (64 Neal St., WC2), for "Eastern Musical Instruments," is probably the only place in Europe you can buy an erh hu, which is, of course, a two-stringed coconut fiddle. It's an amazing place, perfect for gifts for the weird. You can pick up a set of ankle bells or pan pipes for a song.

The Tea House (15A Neal St., WC2). Any shop that's devoted to the British national drink has to be worth a visit, and this one certainly is. There's tea of all kinds on sale, but the most striking feature here is the variety of teapots available—classic ones, copies of 17th-century ones, even pots that caricature the famous. It's a great place to find a really unusual gift.

Jewelry **Asprey's** (165–169 New Bond St., W1) has been described as the "classiest and most luxurious shop in the world." It offers a range of exquisite jewelry and gifts, both antique and modern. If you're in the market for a six-branched Georgian candelabrum or a six-carat emerald and diamond brooch, you won't be disappointed.

All that glisters at **Butler and Wilson** (20 South Molton St., W1) isn't gold. This store is cleverly designed to set off its irresistible costume jewelry to the very best advantage—against a dramatic black background. It has some of the best displays in town, and keeps very busy marketing silver, diamanté, French gilt, and pearls by the truckload. Also at 189 Fulham Road, SW3.

Garrard (112 Regent St., W1). Garrard's connections with the royal family go back to 1722, and they are still responsible for keeping the Crown Jewels in glittering condition. But they are also family jewelers, and offer an enormous range of items in jewelry or silver, from antique to modern. Prince Charles bought Diana her engagement ring here.

Theo Fennell (177 Fulham Rd., SW3). Blue-blooded Fennell's pieces are instantly recognizable—he designs exquisitely detailed miniatures, and covetable jewelry (in gold studded with precious stones) that is reminiscent of the ecclesiastical.

Linen **The Irish Linen Co.** (35–36 Burlington Arcade, W1) is a tiny store bursting with crisp, embroidered linen for the table, the bed, and the nose. Exquisite handkerchiefs should be within reach of everyone's pocket.

Prints **Grosvenor Prints** (28–32 Shelton St., WC2). Shelton Street lies in the tangle of streets northwest of Covent Garden, where many attractive stores have established themselves. Grosvenor Prints sells antiquarian prints, but with an emphasis on views and architecture of London—and dogs! It's an eccentric collection, and the prices range widely, but the stock is so odd that you are bound to find something interesting and unusual to meet both your budget and your taste.

Department Stores

We begin with our favorite, **Liberty** (200 Regent St., W1), easily the most splendid store on Regent Street, and one of London's most attractive. Liberty is a labyrinthine building, full of nooks and crannies, all stuffed with goodies like a dream of an eastern bazaar. Famous principally for its fabrics, it also has an Oriental department, rich with color; men's wear that tends to the traditional; and women's wear that stresses the chic and recherché. It is a store hard to resist, where you may well find an original gift—

especially one made from those classic Liberty prints.

Ten blocks west on Oxford Street—crowded blocks in the middle of the day or at sale time—lies **Selfridges** (400 Oxford St., W1). This giant, bustling store is London's upscale version of Macy's. It has virtually everything you could want for the home and the family. There's a food hall catering to every taste, and a frenetic cosmetics department that seems to perfume the air the whole length of Oxford Street. In recent years, Selfridges has made a specialty of high-profile popular designer fashion. Even more important for the visitor to town, there's a branch of the London Tourist Board on the premises, a theater ticket counter, and a branch of Thomas Cook, the travel agent, in the basement.

Harrods (87 Brompton Rd., SW1) is one of the world's most famous department stores, and is currently owned by an Egyptian family. Harrods lives up to its motto, *Omnia Omnibus Ubique*—everything, for everyone, everywhere. Harrods is not so unabashedly sumptuous as in times past (nor so peaceful!). Visit especially the astounding food halls to see the extensive selections, the elaborate displays—the seafood arrangements, in particular, are stunning—and the lovely floor, wall, and ceiling tiles.

Street Markets

Street markets are mainly a weekend pastime, and, as many of them are open on Sunday morning, they provide something to do on a day that can be extremely dull and dreary in London. A wander through one of the markets, followed by a good Sunday lunch, then an afternoon in a park or by the river, makes a classic London way of cheering up the sabbath.

Camden Lock Market (NW1). Even though its character has changed along with its development into something scrubbed and touristy, this remains just the place to pick up an unusual and inexpensive gift, and it's still a picturesque and pleasant area to wander around, with its cobbled courtyards and the attractive lock itself. There's an antiques market here on Saturday and Sunday, though the individual craft shops are open during the week as well. It does get horribly crowded on weekends. *Take the tube or #24 or #29 bus to Camden Town. Shops open Tues.–Sun. 9:30–5:30, stalls on weekends 8–6.*

Portobello Market (Portobello Rd., W11). Saturday is the best day to search the stalls for treasure in the way of silverware, curios, porcelain, and jewelry. There are 1,500 dealers, meaning that bargains are still possible, especially very early. Saturdays are always crowded, and there are street entertainers and an authentic hustle-and-bustle atmosphere. You'll find that the first section of the market that you come to has the highest-quality merchandise (and the highest prices), while the farther you walk—and it spreads a long way—the more bric-a-brac you see. At the Westway (elevated road), the flea market takes over. *Take a #52 bus or the tube to Ladbroke Grove or Notting Hill Gate. Fruit and vegetables Mon.–Wed. and Fri. 8–5, Thurs. 8–1; antiques Fri. 8–3; both on Sat. 6–5.*

Spitalfields (Brushfield St., E1). Until it eventually becomes shops and offices, the developers of Camden Lock have got hold of the old three-acre indoor fruit market near Petticoat Lane and installed food, crafts and clothes stalls, cafés, performance and sports facilities, and a city farm. *Liverpool St., Aldgate, or Aldgate East tubes are the closest. Open weekdays 11–3, Sun. 9–3.*

VAT Refunds

To the eternal fury of Britain's storekeepers, who struggle under cataracts of paperwork, Britain is afflicted with a 17½% Value Added Tax. Foreign visitors, however, need not pay VAT if they take advantage of the Personal Export Scheme. Almost all of the larger stores have export departments that will be able to give you all the help you need.

Clothing Sizes

Men Suit and shirt sizes in the United Kingdom and the Republic of Ireland are the same as U.S. sizes.

Women *Dresses and Coats*	U.S.	4	6	8	10	12	14	16
	U.K./Ireland	6	8	10	12	14	16	18
Blouses and Sweaters	U.S.	30	32	34	36	38	40	42
	U.K./Ireland	32	34	36	38	40	42	44
Shoes	U.S.	4	5	6	7	8	9	10
	U.K./Ireland	2	3	4	5	6	7	8

4 Dining

In Britain, as in so many countries, not least the United States, the adage "you live to eat, not eat to live" is now a passionately held credo. Whatever your personal version of this creed, it is likely to find satisfaction in London. It cannot necessarily be said that your purse will be as happy as your stomach. But, however impoverished, the average Londoner these days views eating out as something you do when you're hungry, not just when you're celebrating—and, especially away from the center, there are many affordable places to feed that attitude. You're more likely to find Thai, Mediterranean, South Indian, Cal-Ital, French brasserie, or even the style you might call "London," which draws from all those cuisines, than the once-ubiquitous greasy-spoon fare. In fact, quite a few former greasy spoons have taken to opening evenings, wearing tablecloths, and serving, say, the owners' native Thai food. They're not listed here because they're too far off the beaten track, but you can amuse yourself instead trying to work out where, these days, French cuisine ends and "New British" begins.

Many London restaurants have set-lunch menus that are half the price of their à la carte ones. This makes dining in some of the very fanciest eating places within the budget of almost any visitor. The one thing to be careful of is that you don't hike up the cost with the bar check.

A serious problem in dining in London is that it is difficult to do so on Sundays or late at night, and all but impossible over Christmas and New Year's. You should always check if a restaurant is open on Sunday; it could save you a wasted journey.

A law obliges all British restaurants to display their prices, including VAT (sales tax), outside their establishments. Most do so now, and if you are on a tight budget, it's wise to read carefully. Look for the hidden extras such as service, cover, and minimum charge that are usually at the bottom in fine print.

Highly recommended restaurants are indicated by a star ★.

Category	Cost*
Very Expensive	£40 and up
Expensive	£25–£40
Moderate	£15–£25
Inexpensive	under £15

per person without VAT, service, or drinks

Mayfair

Very Expensive
French/ Traditional English
★

The Connaught. This restaurant has a charming and very grand mahogany-paneled, velvet-upholstered, and crystal-chandeliered dining room. Waiters wear tails, tables must be booked far in advance, and prices are fearsome; but this remains one of London's most respected traditional restaurants. Famed French chef Michel Bourdin remains in charge of the kitchens after many years. This is the place for game—venison, guinea fowl, pigeon (not local birds . . .)— presented with traditional trimmings or perhaps with some confection of wild mushrooms. "Luncheon dishes" change according to the day of the week (if this is Friday, it must be oxtail) and are not as exorbitant as they seem at first, since the price includes a starter and dessert. The Connaught is by no means a fashionable place, but it is never out of fashion. *Carlos Pl., W1, tel. 071/499–7070. Jacket and tie required. Reservations advised at least 1 week in advance. MC. Closed weekends and national holidays.*

French
★

Four Seasons. One of Great Britain's great hotel dining rooms, the Four Seasons has won many accolades for Bruno Loubet's modernized Cuisine de Terroir (sautéed mullet with veal jus; poached pear with Chartreuse parfait and raspberry coulis) served in the utmost opulence. Prices are daunting, but lunch is a relative bargain. Service is spectacularly attentive and *very* formal. (*See also* Bistrot Bruno in Soho, *below.*) *Inn on the Park, Hamilton Place, Park La., W1, tel. 071/499–0888. Jacket and tie required. Reservations required at least 2 days in advance. AE, DC, MC, V.*

★

Le Gavroche. Albert Roux has handed the toque

to his son, Michel, who has yet to regain the third Michelin star that was dropped in '93. But many still consider this London's finest restaurant. The excellent service and the discreetly sumptuous decor complement the positively Lucullan *haute cuisine*—seafood velouté with champagne, lobster roasted with cepes and rosemary. The dining room is comfortable and serious, hung with oil paintings, and decorated in a restful dark green. Again, the set lunch is relatively affordable. In fact, it's the only way to eat here if you don't have a generous expense account at your disposal—as most patrons do. *43 Upper Brook St., W1, tel. 071/408-0881. Jacket and tie required. Reservations advised at least 1 week in advance. AE, DC, MC, V. Closed weekends, 10 days at Christmas, national holidays.*

Expensive **The Greenhouse.** Tucked away behind the May-
British fair mansions in a cute, cobbled mews is this elegant salon for people who like their food big and strong. You sit among extravagant topiary and men in ties to partake of Gary Rhodes' much-praised British food. Alone, he handles the P.R. for faggots (a type of meatball, once reviled) and braised oxtails; but he invents new things, too, like smoked eel risotto, and he is the master of the stew—venison and bacon in red wine, perhaps. This is the place for stodgy, sticky English desserts like bread-and-butter pudding and steamed syrup sponge. *27A Hay's Mews, W1, tel. 071/499-3331. Dress: smart. Reservations required. AE, DC, MC, V. Closed Sat. lunch, Sun. dinner, Christmas.*

Irish **Mulligans.** You'd think there'd be more Emerald
★ Isle cooking in London, but it is a very rare commodity, especially done this well. Mulligans is straight out of Dublin, down to the draught Guinness and copies of *The Irish Times* in the upstairs bar. Traditional dishes like steak, Guinness and oyster pie, and Irish stew avoid heaviness while retaining flavor, and the succulent black pudding, served with celeriac and apple, is the best in town. *13–14 Cork St., W1, tel. 071/409-1370. Dress: smart casual. Reservations advised. AE, MC, V. Closed Sat. lunch, Sun. dinner, Dec. 25–26, Jan. 1.*

Moderate
Mediterranean

Zoe. Handy for West End shopping, this two-level place serves two-level food—proper dinners downstairs in a sunlit basement of jazzy colors; and posh cocktails, coffee, and sandwiches ("hot spicy pork with prunes and crispy bacon" is typical) upstairs. It's the newest Antony Worrall Thompson place (*see* Bistrot 190 in South Kensington, *below*) and so features the trademark heartiness. The schizophrenic restaurant menu is half smart "City" dishes (corn crab cakes, poached eggs, hollandaise, and wilted greens), half huge "Country" ensembles (poached ham, parsley sauce, pease pudding, and hot potato salad), most offered in two sizes, rendering decisions impossible. *St. Christopher's Pl., W1, tel. 071/224–1122. Dress: casual. Reservations advised. AE, DC, MC, V. Closed Sat. lunch, Sun. (bar open 7 days), Christmas.*

Modern British

Criterion. This palatial neo-Byzantine mirrored marble hall, which first opened in 1874, is now back on the map. When the huge blue-lit glass clock says 3 PM, it's teatime (£6.50); otherwise you can choose from the modish Cal-Ital brasserie menu: roast garlic squid with lemon oil, herb-baked salmon on cucumber "spaghetti," passion fruit pound cake, or pink grapefruit granita. This is a very welcome oasis in the Piccadilly desert. *Piccadilly Circus, W1, tel. 071/925–0909. Dress: casual. Reservations advised. AE, DC, MC, V. Closed Christmas.*

Inexpensive
American

The Hard Rock Café. People (especially tourists) stand in line for hours to get into this huge, split-level room with ceiling fans, pool lamps, long tables, and ear-splitting rock music. Favorites include BLT sandwiches, ice-cream sodas, and calorific desserts. The hamburgers and steaks are top quality. *150 Old Park La., W1, tel. 071/629–0382. Dress: informal. No reservations. V. Closed Dec. 24–26.*

Mexican

Down Mexico Way. Many of London's proliferating Mexican joints serve horrid food, but this one's been good since the management changed in late '91. The fine lumpy guacamole is fresh, not factory-packed, and amongst the usual tortillas and burritos are a few adventurous numbers like fish in almond-chili sauce, with sides of cheese and jalapeño muffins or spiced spinach. Look for the beautiful Spanish ceramic tiles and avoid evenings if you want a quiet night out. *25 Swallow St., W1, tel. 071/437–9895. Dress: casual. Reservations advised. AE, MC, V. Closed Dec. 25–26.*

St. James's

Very Expensive *Traditional English* **Wilton's.** The most traditional of traditional British fare (turtle soup, seasonal game, "savouries," sherry trifle) is served in Edwardian surroundings. The oysters are the best you'll find anywhere in London—all the seafood arrives fresh up to four times a day—and there's a separate marble-topped oyster bar at which to sample them, preferably with a glass of champagne. *55 Jermyn St., SW1, tel. 071/629–9955. Jacket and tie required. Reservations advised 2 days in advance. AE, DC, MC, V. Closed Sat. lunch, Sun., last week in July and first 2 weeks in Aug., 10 days at Christmas.*

Expensive *Modern British* **Quaglino's.** Sir Terence Conran—of Bibendum and Pont de la Tour fame (*see below*)—lavished £2.5 million doing up this famous pre–World War II haunt of the rich, bored, and well-connected. The gigantic sunken restaurant boasts a glamorous staircase, "Crustacea Altar," small dance floor, and large bar. The food is, of course, fashionably pan-European, with plenty of small fowl (duck magret with olives and noodles), game (rabbit with prosciutto and herbs), and seafood (crab with mirin and soy, roast crayfish, plateaux de fruits de mer, etc., etc.). Desserts come from somewhere between the Paris bistro and the English nursery (raspberry sablé, parkin pudding with butterscotch sauce), and wine from the Old World and the New, at modest prices. *16 Bury St., SW1, tel. 071/930–6767. Dress: smart casual. Reservations required. AE, DC, MC, V. Closed Christmas.*

Moderate *French* **Café Fish.** Just to the east of St James's proper, this cheerful, bustling restaurant has a wonderful selection of fish (shark and turbot join the trout, halibut, salmon, and monkfish, some of which is brought daily from Normandy), arranged on the menu according to cooking method: chargrilled, steamed, *meunière.* There are also several *plats du jour*, some classics of fish cuisine like *bouillabaisse* and *moules marinières,* and a *plateau de fruits de mer* straight out of a Paris brasserie. A delicious little quenelle of smoked fish paté is served with crusty bread to help you order. Downstairs is an informal wine bar with a smaller selection of dishes. *39 Panton St., SW1, tel. 071/930–3999. Dress: informal. Reservations advised. AE, DC, MC, V. Closed Sat. lunch, Sun., Dec. 25–26, Jan. 1.*

Inexpensive
Traditional
English

The Fountain. At the back of Fortnum and Mason's is this old-fashioned restaurant, frumpy and popular as a boarding school matron, serving delicious light meals, toasted snacks, sandwiches, and ice-cream sodas. During the day, go for the Welsh rarebit or cold game pie; in the evening, a no-frills fillet steak is a typical option. Just the place for afternoon tea and ice cream sundaes after the Royal Academy or Bond Street shopping, or for pretheater meals. *181 Piccadilly, W1, tel. 071/734–4938. Dress: informal. Reservations accepted for dinner only. AE, DC, MC, V. Closed Sun., national holidays.*

Soho

Expensive
Modern
British
★

Alastair Little. Little is one of London's most original chefs, drawing inspiration from practically everywhere—Thailand, Japan, Scandinavia, France—and bringing it off brilliantly. His restaurant is starkly modern, so all attention focuses on the menu, which changes not once but twice daily in order to take advantage of the best ingredients. There will certainly be fish, but other than that it's hard to predict. Anyone truly interested in food will not be disappointed. *49 Frith St., W1, tel. 071/734–5183. Dress: informal. Reservations advised. No credit cards. Closed weekends, national holidays, 2 weeks at Christmas, 3 weeks in Aug.*

Moderate
French

Soho Soho. The ground floor is a lively café bar with a rotisserie, while upstairs is a more formal and expensive restaurant. Inspiration comes from Provence, both in the vivid and flavorful food and the decor with its murals, primary colors, and pale ocher terra-cotta floor tiles. The Rotisserie serves omelettes, salads, charcute-

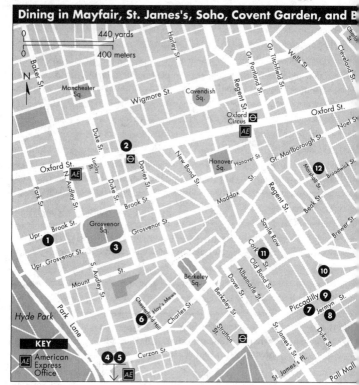

Dining in Mayfair, St. James's, Soho, Covent Garden, and B

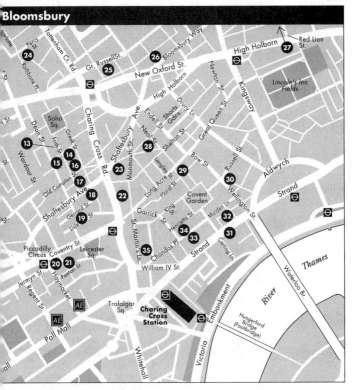

Bloomsbury

rie, and cheeses, plus a handful of bistro dishes like Toulouse sausages with fries; herbed, grilled poussin; and tarte tatin. Or you can stay in the café-bar and have just a kir or a beer. *11–13 Frith St., W1, tel. 071/494–3491. Dress: casual. Reservations advised upstairs. AE, DC, MC, V. Closed Sun., Sat. lunch upstairs, Dec. 25–26, Jan. 1.*

Chinese **Fung Shing.** This comfortable, cool green restaurant is a cut above the Lisle/Wardour Street crowd in both service and ambience, as well as in food. The usual Chinatown options are supplemented by some exciting dishes. Salt-baked chicken, served on or off the bone with an accompanying bowl of intense broth, is essential, and the adventurous might try intestines—deep-fried cigarette-shaped morsels, which are far more delicious than you'd think. *15 Lisle St., WC2, tel. 071/437–1539. Dress: casual. Reservations suggested. AE, DC, MC, V. Closed Dec. 25.*

French **Bistrot Bruno.** Bruno is Bruno Loubet, who
★ earned three Michelin stars at the Four Seasons (*see* Mayfair, *above*) and may be the most dedicated and original chef in London. Here he does everything but cook, but the menu is unmistakably his work, dotted with bits of animals you wouldn't want in your freezer, which in his hands become balanced, beautiful Cuisine du Terroir dishes. His Fromage de téte, or brawn (a paté from the Lorraine made from pig's head in aspic), or tripes niçoise (cow's stomach) may not sound appetizing, but on the plate, they are. Cowards can order scallops on puff pastry or duck leg confit with crushed potato and cepe sauce, then an iced meringue and cherry slice. Coffee arrives with mini-sorbets encased in chocolate. *63 Frith St., W1, tel. 071/734–4545. Dress: smart casual. Reservations required. MC, V. Closed Sat. lunch, Sun., Christmas.*

Mediterranean **dell'Ugo.** A three-floor Mediterranean café-restaurant from the stable of Antony Worrall Thompson (*see* Bistrot 190 in South Kensington, *below*). You can choose light fare—bruschetta loaded with marinated vegetables, mozzarella, parmesan etc., Tuscan soups, and country bread—or feast on wintry, warming one-pot ensembles and large platefuls of sunny dishes like spicy sausages and white bean casserole with onion confit. Fortunately, trendiness doesn't interfere with pleasure here. *56 Frith St., W1, tel. 071/734–8300. Dress: informal. Reservations required for restaurant, not taken for café. AE, MC, V. Closed Sun., Christmas.*

Thai **Bahn Thai.** Many people find this the best of London's many Thai restaurants (you can see at least four others from the door), though the gloomy decor is nothing to write home about. An immensely long menu features little chili symbols for the nervous of palate, plus easy options like chargrilled poussin marinated in honey and spices with a plum dipping sauce. Other Thai dishes are well explained. Wine, by the way, is not a great accompaniment to this food; beer is better. *21A Frith St., W1, tel. 071/437–8504. Dress: casual. Reservations advised for dinner. AE, MC, V. Closed Dec. 25–26.*

Inexpensive **New World.** A cavernous dim sum palace—prob-
Chinese ably the best-known one in London's small Chinatown—serving from trollies between 11 and 6 daily. Demanding gourmets might not enjoy. *1 Gerrard Pl., W1, tel. 071/734–0677. Dress: informal. Reservations not necessary (700 seats). AE, DC, MC, V. Closed Christmas.*

Vegetarian **Crank's.** This is a popular vegetarian chain (there are other branches at Covent Garden, Great Newport Street, Adelaide Street, Tottenham Street, and Barrett Street), bought out by the management in 1992, and now serving more up-to-date meatless meals than the 60s menu that made their name. They remain always crowded, and irritatingly, insist on closing at 8. *8 Marshall St., W1, tel. 071/437–9431. Dress: informal. AE, DC, MC, V. Closed Sun., national holidays.*

Covent Garden

Very **Savoy Grill.** The grill continues in the first rank
Expensive of power dining locations. Politicians, newspa-
French/ per barons, and tycoons like the comforting food
Traditional and impeccably discreet and attentive service in
English the low-key, yew-panelled salon. On the menu, an omelet Arnold Bennett (with cheese and smoked fish) is perennial, as is beef Wellington

on Tuesday and roast Norfolk duck on Friday. Playgoers can split their theater menu, eating part of their meal before the show, the rest after. *Strand, WC2, tel. 071/836–4343. Jacket and tie required. Reservations essential for lunch, and for Thurs.–Sat. dinner. AE, DC, MC, V. Closed Sat. lunch, Sun.*

Expensive
Chinese
★

Now & Zen. This spectacular restaurant, with its audacious shop-window front, glass pavement, and glass waterfall connecting the three floors, would be worth patronizing for the visuals alone. The food more than matches up, since this is one of London's several Zens—ultra-chic Chinese restaurants that practice the creed of freshness, regional dishes, minimal sodium, and no MSG. Menu notes without capital letters encourage balanced ordering—a fried dish to accompany a steamed one; sushi, perhaps, from the short Japanese menu first, or coriander (cilantro) and cuttlefish (squid) cakes. Waitering here is an art form. Tiny, perfectly formed, immaculately black-clad people wrap crispy Szechuan duck pancakes with one hand behind their back. Downstairs in the Lower Deck, you can pay a set price and order all night from a list of 50 small dishes, like Thai chicken with port wine or coriander prawn croquettes. *4A Upper St. Martin's La., WC2, tel. 071/497–0376. Dress: smart casual. Reservations advised. AE, DC, MC, V. Closed Dec. 25–26, Jan. 1.*

International
★

The Ivy. This seems to be everybody's favorite restaurant—everybody who works in the media or the arts, that is. In a Deco dining room with blinding white tablecloths, and Hodgkins and Paolozzis on the walls, the celebrated and the wannabes eat Caesar salad, roast grouse, shrimp gumbo, braised oxtail, and rice pudding with Armagnac prunes or sour-cherry sorbet. *1 West St., WC2, tel. 071/836–4751. Dress: casual but neat. Reservations advised. AE, DC, MC, V. Closed Christmas.*

Italian
★

Orso. The Italian brother of Joe Allen's *(see below)*—a basement restaurant with the same snappy staff and a glitzy clientele of showbiz types and hacks. The Tuscan-style menu changes every day, but always includes excellent pizza and pasta dishes, plus entrees based perhaps on grilled rabbit or roast sea bass and first courses of roquette (arugula) with shaved parmesan or deep-fried zucchini flowers stuffed with ricotta. Food here is never boring, much like the place itself. *27 Wellington St., WC2, tel. 071/240–5269. Dress: casual but neat. Reservations required. No credit cards. Closed Dec. 25–26.*

Traditional English **Rules.** A London institution—an Edwardian restaurant that was a great favorite of Lily Langtry's, among others. After decades the restaurant remains interesting for its splendid period atmosphere, but annoying for its slow service. For a main dish, try the seasonal entrées on the list of daily specials, which will, no doubt, include fish or game (venison is disconcertingly called 'deer'); for a dessert you can't do better than a homemade whiskey-and-ginger ice cream. *35 Maiden La., WC2, tel. 071/836–5314. Dress: casual but neat. Reservations advised at least 1 day in advance. AE, DC, MC, V. Closed Christmas.*

Moderate British **Porters.** Good British food (really), an Olde Worlde public house interior, a nob owner (the Earl of Bradford), and a reasonable check—no wonder Americans invariably like this place. Pies star on the menu—lamb-and-apricot or chicken-and-chili alongside the traditional fish or steak-and-kidney—with steamed sponges and custard for afters. The budget alternative to Rules. *17 Henrietta St., WC2, tel. 071/836–6466. Dress: casual. Reservations required for weekend dinner. AE, MC, V. Closed Christmas.*

American **Joe Allen's.** This New York–clone basement res-
★ taurant, located behind the Strand Palace Hotel, is a great place to spot stage and screen personalities. The ribs these days come with trendy wilted greens and black-eyed peas, but you can still get burgers and fries and brownies and ice cream, and if you eat after 9, you'll be entertained by a pianist—if you can hear through the din. *13 Exeter St., WC2, tel. 071/836–0651. Dress: casual. Reservations required. No credit cards. Closed Easter, Dec. 25–26.*

Italian **Bertorelli's.** Right across from the stage door of
★ the Royal Opera House, Bertorelli's is quietly

chic, the food better than ever now that Maddalena Bonnino (formerly of 192) is in charge. Poached cotechino sausage with lentils; monkfish ragout with fennel, tomato and olives; and garganelli with French beans, cob nuts, and parmesan are typical dishes. Downstairs is a very relaxed inexpensive wine bar serving a simpler menu of pizza, pasta, salads, and a few big dishes and daily specials. *44A Floral St., WC2, tel. 071/836-3969. Dress: smart casual. Reservations required for restaurant; advised downstairs for dinner. AE, DC, MC, V. Closed Christmas.*

Inexpensive **Café Flo.** This useful brasserie serves the bar-
French gain "Idée Flo"—soup or salad, *steak-frites* or *poisson-frites*, and coffee—a wide range of French café food, breakfast, wines, *tartes*, espresso, fresh orange juice, simple set-price weekend menus . . . everything for the francophile on a budget. There are branches in Hampstead, Islington, Fulham, and Kensington. *51 St. Martin's La., WC2, tel. 071/836-8289. Dress: casual. Reservations advised. MC, V. Closed Dec. 25, Jan. 1.*

Vegetarian **Food for Thought.** This simple basement restau-
★ rant (no liquor license) seats only 50 and is extremely popular, so you'll almost always find a line of people down the stairs. The menu—stir-fries, casseroles, salads, and desserts—changes every day, and each dish is freshly made; there's no microwave. *31 Neal St., WC2, tel. 071/836-0239. Dress: informal. No reservations. No credit cards. Closed after 8 PM, 2 weeks at Christmas, national holidays.*

Bloomsbury

Expensive **The White Tower.** Barely changed in 50 years,
Greek the White Tower is the most elegant Greek restaurant in London, with portraits on the walls (Lord Byron upstairs), glass partitions between the tables, and an entertainingly rhapsodic menu. Dishes range from the traditional—*taramasalata*—to the more creative—roast duckling stuffed with crushed wheat. *1 Percy St., W1, tel. 071/636-8141. Jacket and tie required. Reservations required. AE, DC, MC, V.*

Closed weekends, national holidays, 3 weeks in Aug., 1 week at Christmas.

Moderate **The Museum Street Café.** This tiny restaurant
Modern near the British Museum serves a limited selec-
British tion of impeccably fresh dishes, intelligently
and plainly cooked by the two young owners.
The evening menu might feature grilled, maize-
fed chicken with pesto, followed with a rich
chocolate cake; at lunchtime you might choose a
sandwich of Stilton on walnut bread and a big
bowl of soup. Bring your own wine. *47 Museum
St., WC1, tel. 071/405–3211. Dress: casual. Reservations required for dinner. No credit cards.
Closed weekends, public holidays.*

Inexpensive **Wagamama.** London's gone wild for Japanese
Japanese noodles in this big basement. It's high-tech
(your order is taken on a hand-held computer)
and high-volume—there are always crowds,
with which you share wooden refectory tables,
so the noise level is inevitably high. You can
choose ramen in or out of soup, topped with
sliced meats or tempura; or "raw energy" dishes—rice, curries, tofu, and so on. *4 Streatham
St., WC1, tel. 071/323–9223. Dress: casual. No
reservations. No credit cards. Closed Christmas.*

Seafood **The North Sea Fish Restaurant.** This is the place
★ for the British national dish of fish-and-chips—
battered and deep-fried whitefish with thick
fries shaken with salt and vinegar. It's a bit
tricky to find—three blocks south of St. Pancras
station, down Judd Street. Only freshly caught
fish is served, and you can order it grilled—
though that would defeat the object. You can
take out or eat in. *7–8 Leigh St., WC1, tel. 071/
387–5892. Dress: informal. Reservations advised. AE, DC, MC, V. Closed Sun., national
holidays, Christmas.*

South Kensington

Very **Bibendum.** Bibendum is in the reconditioned
Expensive Michelin House, with its Art Deco decorations
French and brilliant stained glass, Conran Shop, and
★ Oyster Bar. For some years now it has been
home to Simon Hopkinson's enormous talent.
He is famous for preparing simple dishes per-
fectly. Thus you can order herrings with sour

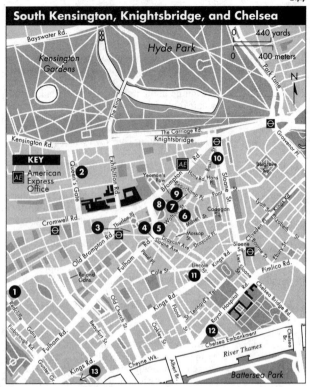

South Kensington, Knightsbridge, and Chelsea

Bibendum, **4**

Bistrot 190, **2**

Caravela, **7**

Chelsea Kitchen, **11**

Chutney Mary, **13**

Daquise, **3**

Joe's Café, **5**

La Tante Claire, **12**

Lou Pescadou, **1**

Luba's Bistro, **9**

St. Quentin, **8**

Stockpot, **10**

Waltons, **6**

cream, a risotto, or leeks vinaigrette followed by steak au poivre or the perfect boeuf bourguignon, or you might try brains or tripe as they ought to be cooked. The set-price menu at lunchtime is money well spent. *Michelin House, 81 Fulham Rd., SW3, tel. 071/581–5817. Dress: informal. Reservations required. MC, V. Closed Sun.*

Moderate
French
★
Lou Pescadou. Walking into this little restaurant is like stepping into the south of France. The staff is emphatically French and, although fish is the specialty—*petite bouillabaisse* (fish soup) or red mullet poached in tarragon sauce— there are meat dishes, too, sometimes very unusual ones, like delicate and delicious braised *cervelles*—brains. *241 Old Brompton Rd., SW5, tel. 071/370–1057. Dress: informal. No reservations. AE, DC, MC, V. Closed Aug., Christmas.*

Mediterranean
Bistrot 190. Chef-restaurateur and popular guy Antony Worrall Thompson dominates this town's medium-priced eating scene with his happy, hearty food from Southern Europe (liver and wild mushroom terrine; chargrilled squid with red and green salsa; lemon tart) in raucous hardwood-floor-and-art settings. This place, the first of four, opened in '91 and is handy to museum or Albert Hall excursions. The others are the next-door Downstairs at 190, dell'Ugo in Soho (*see above*), and Zoe on St. Christopher's Place, off Oxford Street (*see Mayfair, above*). *190 Queen's Gate, SW7, tel. 071/581–5666. Dress: smart casual. No reservations. AE, DC, MC, V. Closed Sat. lunch, Sun., Dec. 25–26, Jan. 1.*

Inexpensive
Polish
Daquise. This venerable and well-loved Polish café by the tube station is incongruous in this neighborhood, since it's neither style-conscious nor expensive. Fill your stomach without emptying your pocketbook (or, it must be said, overstimulating your taste buds) on *bigos* (sauerkraut with garlic sausage and mushrooms), stuffed cabbage and cucumber salad, or just coffee and cakes. *20 Thurloe St., SW7, tel. 071/589–6117. Dress: casual. Reservations advised weekend dinner. No credit cards. Closed Christmas.*

Knightsbridge

Very Expensive
Traditional English

Waltons. Popular with Americans, this formal, sumptuous restaurant has strong color schemes, acres of rich fabrics, and flowers. The cuisine is as rich as the surroundings and, though billed as British, is not so easy to categorize—try the ravioli stuffed with lobster or the steamed red mullet on a fondue of tomatoes and fresh basil. *121 Walton St., SW3, tel. 071/584–0204. Jacket and tie required. Reservations advised. AE, DC, MC, V. Closed Christmas, Dec. 25–26, Jan. 1, and Easter.*

Moderate French

St. Quentin. A very popular slice of Paris, frequented by French expatriates and locals alike. The cuisine is meaty, Gallic, and plain, with some more modern dishes—lime and honey marinated duck breast, for instance, or sweetbreads with a hazelnut sauce. *Tartes* for dessert come from St. Quentin's gourmet food shop, Les Specialités, as do the cheeses. It can become a lot more expensive if you dine à la carte. *243 Brompton Rd., SW3, tel. 071/589–8005. Dress: casual but neat. Reservations advised. AE, DC, MC, V.*

Portuguese

Caravela. This narrow lower-ground-floor place is one of London's few Portuguese restaurants. You can get *Caldo verde* (cabbage soup), *bacalhau* (salt-cured cod), and other typical dishes while listening (on Friday or Saturday) to the national music, fado—desperately sad, songs belted out at thrash-metal volume. *39 Beauchamp Pl., SW3, tel. 071/581–2366. Dress: casual. Reservations advised weekend dinner. AE, DC, MC, V. Closed Sun. lunch, Christmas, Easter.*

Inexpensive International

Stockpot. You'll find speedy service in this large, jolly restaurant, often packed to the brim with young people and shoppers. The food is filling and wholesome: try the Lancashire hot pot, for example, and the apple crumble. *6 Basil St., SW3, tel. 071/589–8627. Dress: informal. Reservations accepted. No credit cards. Closed Christmas, national holidays. Other branches at 40 Panton St., off Leicester Sq. (tel. 071/839–5142); 18 Old Compton St., Soho (tel. 071/287–1066); and 273 King's Rd., Chelsea (tel. 071/823–3175).*

Russian **Luba's Bistro.** Popular for decades: long wooden tables, plain decor, and authentic Russian cooking—chicken Kiev, beef Stroganoff, etc. Bring your own wine. *6 Yeoman's Row, SW3, tel. 071/ 589–2950. Dress: informal. Reservations required. MC, V. Closed Sun., national holidays.*

Chelsea

Very Expensive
French
★
La Tante Claire. Justly famous, but cripplingly expensive. The decor is light and sophisticated, the service impeccable, the French wine list impressive, but the food is the point. From the *carte,* you might choose hot pâté de foie gras on shredded potatoes with a sweet wine and shallot sauce, roast spiced pigeon, or Pierre Koffmann's famous signature dish of pig's feet stuffed with mousse of white meat with sweetbreads and wild mushrooms. As every gourmet expense-accounter knows, the set lunch menu is a genuine bargain. Walk your meal off afterwards along the nearby Thames embankment. *68 Royal Hospital Rd., SW3, tel. 071/352–6045. Jacket and tie required. Reservations advised 3–4 weeks in advance for dinner, 2–3 days for lunch. AE, DC, MC, V. Closed weekends, 2 weeks at Christmas, Jan. 1, 10 days at Easter, 3 weeks in Aug.–Sept.*

Expensive
Anglo-Indian
Chutney Mary. London's first-and-only Anglo-Indian restaurant provides a fantasy version of the British Raj, all giant wicker armchairs and palms. Dishes like Masala roast lamb (practically a whole leg, marinated and spiced) and "Country Captain" (braised chicken with almonds, raisins, chilis, and spices) alternate with the more familiar North Indian dishes like roghan josh (lamb curry). The best choices are certainly the dishes recreated from the kitchens of Indian chefs cooking for English palates back in the old Raj days. For this reason, the all-you-can-eat Sunday buffet is not such a great idea, since it leaves those out. Service is deferential, and desserts, unheard of in tandoori places (kulfi excepted), are worth leaving room for. *535 King's Rd., SW10, tel. 071/351–3113. Dress: smart. Reservations advised. AE, DC, MC, V. Closed Dec. 25 dinner, Dec. 26.*

Modern **Joe's Café.** A stylish brasserie just across the
British road from Bibendum, serving light, chic food to
suit the designer patrons and Designer Patron—he is Joseph Etedgui, the fashion maven
and inventor of '80s matte black. As dishes like
lemon shrimp salad or tagliatelle Nero with
squid suggest, this is not really a café at all, but
a none-too-cheap restaurant. Staff can be
snooty. *126 Draycott Ave., SW3, tel. 071/225–
2217. Dress: casual but neat. Reservations advised. AE, DC, MC, V. Closed Sun. evening, 1
week Christmas.*

Inexpensive **Chelsea Kitchen.** This café has been crowded
International since the '60s with hungry people after hot, filling, and inexpensive food. Expect nothing more
fancy than pasta, omelets, salads, stews, and
casseroles. The menu changes every day. *98
King's Rd., SW3, tel. 071/589–1330. Dress: casual. No reservations. No credit cards. Closed
Christmas.*

Kensington and Notting Hill Gate

Expensive **Boyd's.** Situated under a conservatory dome,
French this stylish, summery, modern restaurant
serves trendy French cuisine—a salad of grilled
chicken or of duck and mango; or a boned roast
quail with apples and wild rice. The menu
changes monthly. *135 Kensington Church St.,
W8, tel. 071/727–5452. Jacket and tie required.
Reservations advised. AE, MC, V. Closed
Mon., Sun., 1 week at Christmas, Easter.*

French/Californian **Clarke's.** There's no choice on the evening menu
★ at Sally Clarke's winning restaurant; her set
dinner features ultrafresh ingredients, plainly
but perfectly cooked, accompanied by home-
baked breads. *124 Kensington Church St., W8,
tel. 071/221–9225. Dress: casual but neat. Reservations required. MC, V. Closed weekends,
public holidays, 2 weeks in Aug.*

Modern **Kensington Place.** A favorite among the local
British glitterati, always packed and noisy. A huge
★ plate-glass window and mural are backdrops to
some of London's most fashionable food—
grilled foie gras with sweet-corn pancake and
baked tamarillo with vanilla ice are perennials.
*201 Kensington Church St., W8, tel. 071/727–
3184. Dress: casual but neat. Reservations ad-*

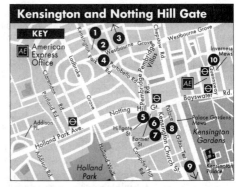

*vised. MC, V. Closed Aug. bank holiday,
Christmas.*

Moderate   **L'Artiste Assoiffé.** Stanley and Sally the parrots
French   will scold you in the bar of this eccentric Victorian house before you proceed to the Cancan room
or the Carousel room to eat. The music is usually
operatic. Pop stars, actors, and royals come here
for the food (fillet steak with dijon mustard;
spinach pancakes with nuts and cheese), but
more for the unique atmosphere. *122 Kensington Park Rd., W11, tel. 071/727–4714. Dress: casual but neat. Reservations required. AE, DC,
MC, V. Closed Sun., national holidays.*

Greek   **Kalamaras.** Here are two small, friendly, authentic Greek restaurants, one "micro" and one
"mega," nearly next door to each other. The
micro, which doesn't have a liquor license, is
cheaper but more cramped than the mega. Try a
plate of *mezze* for starters, and go on to say, ke-
babs and salads. *76–78 Inverness Mews, W2, tel.
071/727–9122. Dress: informal. Reservations
advised. AE, DC, MC, V. Dinner only. Closed
Sun., national holidays.*

Modern   **192.** Upstairs is a noisy wine bar where the local
British   trendies actually live; downstairs is a perennial-
★   ly popular, relaxed restaurant serving Dan
Evans's school-of-Alistair-Little (who began
here) flavorsome cooking. On a menu that
changes twice a day, there are always inventive
salads (like romanesco, broccoli, anchovy, and
gremolata), plus at least one fish (sea bass with
fennel, lemon, and rosemary), and something

unexpected (scallop, chickpea, chorizo, and clam casserole). Since first courses are often more exciting, many people order two of them instead of an entrée. *192 Kensington Park Rd., W11, tel. 071/229-0482. Dress: smart casual. Reservations advised. AE, MC, V. Closed Mon., lunch, public holidays.*

Polish **Wodka.** This smart, modern Polish restaurant is ★ the only one in the world, as far as we know, to serve smart, modern Polish food. It is popular with elegant locals plus a sprinkling of celebs and often has the atmosphere of a dinner party. Alongside the smoked salmon, herring, caviar, and eggplant *blinis*, you might also find venison-and-wild-boar sausages or roast duck with honey sauce. Try the flavored vodkas—warm or chilled. *12 St. Albans Grove, W8, tel. 071/937-6513. Dress: casual but neat. Reservations required for dinner. AE, DC, MC, V. Closed weekend lunch, public holidays.*

Inexpensive **Gate Diner.** Burgers, steak-in-baguette, chef's *American* salad, baked potatoes, potato skins, pecan pie, and ice cream in a split-level, wood-floored room with walls of screen-star photos. Handy for Portobello antiquing. *184A Kensington Park Rd., W11, tel. 071/221-2649. Dress: casual. Reservations advised weekends. MC, V. Closed Christmas.*

International **All Saints.** Trendy, trendy, trendy, and bound to have been eclipsed by now as the place to be seen, but still a useful stop on a Portobello market jaunt. During the day there are croissants, waffles, and danish in the morning, salads, pastas, and sandwiches for lunch. Come the evening it turns into a soul-food/Cajun place—fried chicken and corn bread, good vegetables, little choice. The decor is spartan. *12-14 All Saint's Rd., W11, tel. 071/243-2808. Dress: casual. Reservations required for dinner. MC, DC, V. Closed Sun. dinner, Christmas.*

Seafood **Geales.** This is a cut above your typical fish-and-★ chips joint. The decor is stark but the fish will have been swimming in the sea just a few hours beforehand, even the ones from the Caribbean (fried swordfish is a specialty). Geales is popular with the rich and famous, not just loyal locals. *2 Farmer St., W8, tel. 071/727-7969. Dress: infor-*

Spend your
vacation
touring
castles.
Not train
stations.

Vacation Cars. Vacation Prices. Wherever your destination in Europe, there is sure to be one of more than 1,000 Budget locations nearby. Budget offers considerable values on a wide variety of quality cars, and if you book before you leave the U.S., you'll save even more with a special rate package from the Budget World Travel Plan." For information and reservations, contact your travel consultant or call Budget in the U.S. at **800-472-3325.** Or, while traveling abroad, call a Budget reservation center.

THE SMART MONEY IS ON BUDGET.®

We feature Ford and other fine cars.   *A system of corporate and licensee owned locations.*

MCI brings Europe and America closer together.

Call the U.S. for less with MCI CALL USA®

It's easy and affordable to call home when you use MCI CALL USA!

- Less expensive than calling through hotel operators
- Available from over 80 countries and locations worldwide
- You're connected to English-speaking MCI® Operators
- Even call 800 numbers in the U.S.†

†Regular MCI CALL USA rates apply to 800 number calls.

Call the U.S. for less from these European locations.

Dial the toll-free access number for the country you're calling from.
Give the U.S. MCI Operator the number you're calling and the method of payment: MCI Card, U.S. local phone company card or collect. Your call will be completed!

Austria	022-903-012	Hungary	00*-800-01411	Poland	0*-01-04-800-222
Belgium	078-11-00-12	Ireland	1-800-551-001	Portugal	05-017-1234
Czech/Slovak	00-42-000112	Italy	172-1022	San Marino	172-1022
Denmark	8001-0022	Liechtenstein	155-0222	Spain	900-99-0014
Finland	9800-102-80	Luxembourg	0800-0112	Sweden	020-795-922
France	19*-00-19	Monaco	19*-00-19	Switzerland	155-0222
Germany	0130-0012	Netherlands	06*-022-91-22	United Kingdom	0800-89-0222
Greece	00-800-1211	Norway	050-12912	Vatican City	172-1022

* Wait for 2nd dial tone.
Collect calls not accepted on MCI CALL USA calls to 800 numbers.
Some public phones may require deposit of coin or phone card for dial tone.

Call 1-800-444-3333 in the U.S. to apply for your MCI Card® now!

© MCI International Inc. 1993

mal. *No reservations. MC. Closed Sun., Mon.,
2 weeks at Christmas, 3 weeks in Aug., national
holidays.*

The City

Expensive **Le Pont de la Tour.** Sir Terence Conran's previ-
French ous pièce de résistance (before Quaglino's, that
is) lies across the river, overlooking the bridge
that gives it its name, and so comes into its own
in summer, when the outside tables are heaven.
Inside the "Gastrodrome" (his word) there's a
vintner and baker and deli, a seafood bar, a
brasserie, and this '30s liner-style restaurant,
smart as the captain's table. Fish and seafood
(lobster salad; Baltic herrings in crème fraîche;
roast halibut with aioli), meat and game (venison fillet, port and blueberry sauce; roast veal,
caramelized endive) feature heavily—vegetari-
ans are out of luck. Prune and Armagnac tart or
chocolate terrine could finish a glamorous—and
expensive—meal. By contrast, an impeccable
salade niçoise in the brasserie is about £8. *36D
Shad Thames, Butler's Wharf, SE1, tel. 071/
403–8403. Dress: smart. Reservations required
for lunch, weekend dinner. MC, V. Closed
Christmas.*

Moderate **Quality Chop House.** This was converted from
Traditional one of the most gorgeous "greasy spoon" caffs in
English town, retaining the solid Victorian fittings (including pew-like seats, which you often have to
share). It is not luxurious, but the food is wonderful. It's almost a parody of caff food—
bangers and mash turns out to be home-made
herbed veal sausage with rich gravy, light,
fluffy potato, and vegetables *à point;* egg and
chips (fries) are not remotely greasy. There are
also posh things like salmon fishcakes and steak,
and desserts that change with the seasons. *94
Farringdon Rd., EC1, tel. 071/837–5093. Dress:
casual. Reservations required. No credit cards.
Closed Sat. lunch, Sun. dinner, public holidays.*

Inexpensive **The Eagle.** If the name makes it sound like a
Italian pub, that's because it is a pub, albeit a superior
★ one, with wooden floors, a few sofas, and art on
the walls. It does, however, belong in the "Dining" section by virtue of the amazingly good-

The Eagle, **2**
Le Pont de la
Tour, **1**
Quality Chop
House, **3**

Dining in the City

value nouveau Tuscan food, which you choose
from the blackboard menu (or by pointing) at
the bar. There are about half a dozen dishes, a
pasta and/or risotto always among them. There
are currently quite a few places in London
charging four times the price for remarkably
similar—and no better—food. *159 Farringdon
Rd., EC1, tel. 071/837-1353. Dress: casual. No
reservations. No credit cards. No food served
Sat., Sun. evenings.*

Pubs

Black Friar. You can't miss it—it's the only
wedge-shaped, ornate building with a statue of
a friar on the front as you step out of Blackfriars
tube station! It was built in 1875 and is a tri-
umph of Victorian extravagance, with inlaid
mother-of-pearl, delicate wood-carving, stained
glass, and bronze bas-reliefs of friars. In the
"side chapel" you'll see red marble pillars and a
magnificent mosaic ceiling, plus more friars,
and devils, *and* fairies—all very art nouveau.
There are six kinds of beer on tap. *174 Queen
Victoria St., EC4, tel. 071/236-5650.*
Bunch of Grapes. This popular Victorian (1882)
pub in the heart of Shepherd Market, the vil-
lage-within-Mayfair, just off Piccadilly, attracts a colorful crowd. *16 Shepherd Market,
W1, tel. 071/629-4989.*
Cheshire Cheese (Ye Olde). The mood here is set
by the low ceilings, wooden tables, sawdust
floors, and the 14th-century crypt of Whitefri-
ars' monastery under the cellar bar. It's one of

London's best-loved, most historic pubs. *145 Fleet St., EC4, tel. 071/353–6170.*

The Lamb. Dickens lived close by and, yes, he was a regular here, too (he seems to have spent his life on a pub crawl). It's a jolly, cozy pub, with the original cut-glass Victorian screens. The food is home-cooked, and you can eat or drink outside on the patio. It's crowded in summer. *94 Lamb's Conduit St., WC1, tel. 071/405–0713.*

Lamb and Flag. This 17th-century pub was once known as "The Bucket of Blood," because the upstairs room was used as a ring for bare-knuckle boxing. Now, it's a trendy, friendly, and entirely bloodless pub, serving food (at lunchtime only) and real ale. It's on the edge of Covent Garden, off Garrick Street. *33 Rose St., WC2, tel. 071/836–4108.*

Mayflower. An atmospheric 17th-century riverside inn with exposed beams and a terrace, this is practically the very place from which the Pilgrims set sail for Plymouth Rock. The inn is licenced to sell American postage stamps alongside its superior pub food. *117 Rotherhithe St., SE16, tel. 071/237–4088.*

Museum Tavern. Across the street from the British Museum, this gloriously Victorian pub makes an ideal resting place after the rigors of the culture trail. With lots of fancy glass—etched mirrors and stained glass panels—gilded pillars, and carvings, this heavily restored hostelry once helped Karl Marx to unwind after a hard day in the Library. He could have spent his kapital on any one of six beers available on tap. *49 Great Russell St., WC1, tel. 071/242–8987.*

Prospect of Whitby. Named after a ship, this historic riverside tavern dates back to 1520. Once upon a time it was called "The Devil's Tavern," because of the numbers of low-life criminals—thieves and smugglers—who congregated here. It's ornamented with pewter ware and nautical memorabilia. There's an excellent à la carte menu, as well as good pub food. *57 Wapping Wall, E1, tel. 071/481–1095.*

5 Lodging

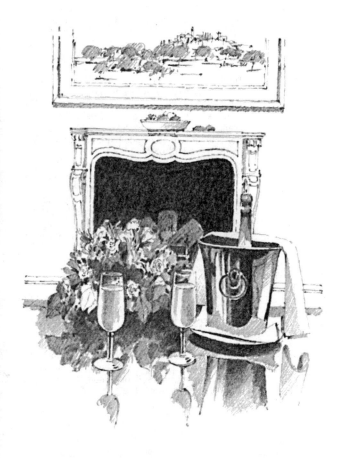

London hotels are among the most expensive in Europe in all grades, and the situation shows no sign of changing in the near future. Our gradings are based on the average room cost, and you should note that in some establishments, especially those in the Very Expensive category, you could pay considerably more—well past the £200 mark in some cases. Like hotels in most other European countries, British hotels are obliged by law to display a tariff at the reception desk. If you have not prebooked, you are strongly advised to study this carefully.

Be sure to make reservations well in advance, as seasonal events, trade shows, or royal occasions can fill hotel rooms for sudden brief periods. However, if you arrive in the capital without a room, the following organizations should be able to help: **Room Centre (U.K.) Ltd.** (Rex House, 4 Regent St., SW1Y 4PE, tel. 071/930–0572); the **British Travel Centre** (12 Regent St., SW1Y 4PQ, tel. 071/730–3400); **Hotel Reservation Centre** (by Platform 8 at Victoria Station, tel. 071/828–1849); and the **London Tourist Board Information Centres** at Heathrow and Victoria Station Forecourt (tel. 071/824–8844 for bookings prepaid by credit card—MC or V).

Highly recommended hotels are indicated by a star ★.

Category	Cost*
Very Expensive	over £160
Expensive	£110–£160
Moderate	£60–£110
Inexpensive	under £60

cost of a double room; VAT included; add service

Mayfair to Regent's Park

Very Expensive ★ **Claridges.** A hotel legend, with one of the world's classiest guest lists. The liveried staff are friendly and not in the least condescending, and the rooms are never less than luxurious. It was founded in 1812, but present decor is either 1930s Art Deco or country-house traditional.

Lodging in Mayfair, St. James's, Soho, and Covent Garden

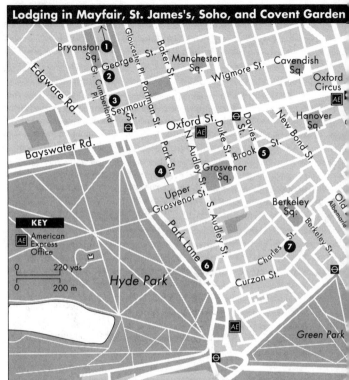

KEY

AE American Express Office

0 ——— 220 yds
0 ——— 200 m

Bryanston Court, **2**

Chesterfield, **7**

Claridges, **5**

The Dorchester, **6**

Dorset Square Hotel, **1**

Edward Lear, **3**

47 Park Sreet, **4**

Hampshire, **9**

Hazlitt's, **8**

The Savoy, **10**

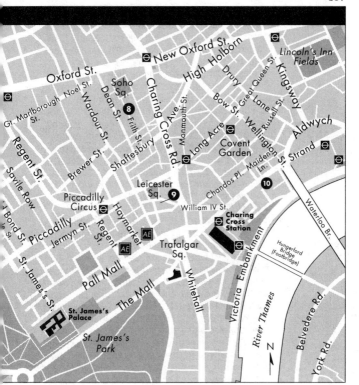

Have a drink in the Foyer lounge (24 hours a day) with its Hungarian mini–orchestra, or retreat to the reading room for perfect quiet, interrupted only by the sound of pages turning. The bedrooms are spacious, as are the bathrooms, with their enormous shower heads and bells (which still work) to summon either "maid" or "valet" from their station on each floor. Beds are handmade and supremely comfortable—the King of Morocco once brought his own, couldn't sleep, and ended up ordering 30 from Claridges to take home. The grand staircase and magnificent elevator are equally impressive. *Brook St., W1A 2JQ, tel. 071/629–8860, fax 071/499–2210. 200 rooms with bath. Facilities: 2 restaurants, lounge (with orchestra), hairdressing, valeting. AE, DC, MC, V.*

★ **The Dorchester.** This hotel, a great London institution, underwent a complete refurbishment that was completed in late 1990 and has now reclaimed its place as one of the world's best hotels. The grand public rooms have always ensured a high profile for this home-away-from-home for the rich and famous; now the bedrooms, with computerized climate control, and the remodeled marble bathrooms, with pool-size tubs and walk-in showers, also measure up to the hotel's exacting standards. There are extra conveniences, too, like portable fax machines and power outlets that convert to 110V, plus a luxury spa with a gym. The Grill is one of London's power dining spots and there are two other swanky restaurants, a bar, and vast acres of the Promenade lounge for tea. Probably no other hotel this opulent manages to be this charming. *Park La., W1A 2HJ, tel. 071/629–8888, fax 071/409–0114. 197 rooms, 55 suites with bath. Facilities: 3 restaurants, bar, lounge, nightclub, health club (no pool), business center, banqueting suites, ballroom, shopping arcade, free in-house movies, CNN, air-conditioning, valeting, theater ticket desk. AE, DC, MC, V.*

★ **47 Park Street.** Secreted back to back with the grand hotels of Park Lane, this dear (in every sense) little all-suite hotel has the best room service in town, with 24-hour food direct from the kitchen of Le Gavroche (*see* Chapter 4). The hotel shares its bar with that poshest of posh dining establishments, too, which means there's a jacket-and-tie requirement for your quiet nightcap. Bathrooms are on the small side, but no other drawbacks are apparent in this fabulously discreet, exquisitely decorated, quiet, relaxed, and homey haven, as long as you can afford it. One woman who could afford it liked it so much that she's still there—three years later. *47 Park St., W1Y 4EB, tel. 071/491–7282, fax 071/491–7281. 52 suites with bath and kitchen. Facilities: lounge, bar (jacket and tie required), private dining room, air-conditioning, satellite TV, fax, VCR on request, shopping, babysitting. AE, DC, MC, V.*

Hampshire. This hotel is in Leicester Square, which often seems to be the real center of London. It's the only place with any life after midnight, being next to all the theaters, big movie houses, and clubs—and so, therefore, is the Hampshire. Though built in 1899 to house the Royal Dental Hospital, virtually all that's left of the original structure is the elegant Edwardian facade, a dignified blend of brick and terracotta. Sadly neglected for some time, it took a £7.5 million restoration to create the impression of luxury and calm that greets you here. A very reliable small chain called Edwardian Hotels was responsible, and the place is done out in their trademark "gracious country house" style, with open fires, dark wood, and, in this one, a fair bit of Chinoiserie. There are six rooms and two suites with four-poster beds, and 42 studios with seating areas and huge, magnificently equipped bathrooms. Try for a room in the front of the hotel, looking over the square, as they are the largest. This is an ideal base for anyone in town on a shopping spree or a theater crawl. *31 Leicester Sq., WC2H 7LH, tel. 071/839–9399, fax 071/930–8122. 124 rooms with bath. Facilities: restaurant, wine bar, bar, satellite TV. AE, DC, MC, V.*

Expensive **Chesterfield.** This former town house of the Earl of Chesterfield is popular with American visitors, many of whom are repeat guests or have links with the English Speaking Union, which has its headquarters next door. It is deep in the heart of Mayfair and has welcoming, wood-and-leather public rooms and spacious bedrooms. The staff is outstandingly pleasant and helpful. *35 Charles St., W1X 8LX, tel. 071/491–2622, fax 071/491–4793. 113 rooms with bath. Facilities: restaurant, in-house movies. AE, DC, MC, V.*

★ **Dorset Square Hotel.** A decade old, this special small hotel off Baker Street was the first of three London addresses for husband and wife Tim and Kit Kemp, an architect and an interior designer. What they did was decant the English country look into a fine pair of Regency town houses, then turn up the volume. Everywhere you look are covetable antiques, edibly rich colors, and ideas *House Beautiful* subscribers will steal. Naturally every room is different, with the first-floor balconied "Coronet" ones the largest (two have grand pianos), and a virtue made of the smallness of the small ones. The marble and mahogany bathrooms have power showers; glossy magazines, a half-bottle of claret, and boxes of vitamin C are complimentary. Instead of minibars guests will find an "honesty bar"—a drinks cabinet—in the small front parlor. There's a reason for the ubiquitous cricket memorabilia: Dorset Square was the first Lord's ground. (Nowadays you can have your drinks served in the garden that still remains.) The Country Manners basement bar/restaurant has cheerful frescoes, chess, backgammon, and a menu more innovative than the name suggests. *39–40 Dorset Sq., NW1 6QN, tel. 071/723–7874, fax 071/724–3328. 37 rooms with bath. Facilities: bar/restaurant, garden, vintage Bentley limousine, 24-hr. room service, air-conditioning. AE, MC, V.*

Moderate **Bryanston Court.** Three Georgian houses have
★ been converted into a hotel in a historic conservation area, a couple of blocks north of Hyde Park and Park Lane. The style is traditional English—open fireplaces, comfortable leather armchairs, oil portraits—though the bedrooms are small and modern, with pink furnishings, creaky floors, and minute bathrooms. Rooms at the back are quieter and face east, so they're bright in the mornings; room 77 is as big as a suite, but being on the lower ground floor typical of London houses, it's dark. This family-run

hotel is excellent value for the area. *56–60 Great Cumberland Pl., W1H 7FD, tel. 071/262–3141, fax 071/262–7248. 56 rooms with bath. Facilities: bar, lounge, restaurant. AE, DC, MC, V.*

Edward Lear. One-time home of writer/artist Edward Lear (famous for his nonsense verse), this good-value hotel has an inviting entranceway leading to a black-and-white tiled hall. Rooms vary enormously in size, with some family rooms very spacious indeed and others barely big enough to get out of bed (avoid #14); rooms at the back are quieter. It's a friendly place with a lot of repeat customers, but there are no hotel-type facilities (although if you want a jacket pressed you're welcome to borrow the iron), and the only public area is the light and pleasant breakfast room. The management is very proud of the English breakfasts—they use the same butcher as the queen. *28–30 Seymour St., W1H 5WD, tel. 071/402–5401, fax 071/706–3766. 30 rooms, 15 with bath. V.*

Soho and Covent Garden

Very Expensive
★

The Savoy. This historic, grand, late-Victorian hotel is beloved by the international influential, now as ever. Like the other Savoy Group hotels, it boasts handmade beds and staff who are often graduates of its famous training school. Its famous Grill (*see* Chapter 4) has the premier power lunch tables; it hosted Elizabeth Taylor's first honeymoon in one of its famous river-view rooms; and it poured the world's first martini in its equally famous American Bar—haunted by Hemingway, Fitzgerald, Gershwin, *et al.* And does it measure up to this high profile? Absolutely. The impeccably maintained, spacious, elegant, bright, and comfortable rooms are furnished with antiques and serviced by valets. A room facing the Thames costs an arm and a leg and requires an early booking, but there are few better views in London. Bathrooms have original fittings, with the same sunflower-size shower heads as at Claridges. The only serious gap in facilities was filled last year with a rooftop health club. Though the Savoy is as grand as they come, the air is tinged with a certain naughtiness, which goes down well with Hollywood types. *Strand, WC2R 0EU, tel. 071/836–*

4343, fax 071/240–6040. 202 rooms with bath. Facilities: hairdressing, florist, theater ticket desk, 3 restaurants, 2 bars, valeting, free in-house movies. AE, DC, MC, V.

Moderate
★ **Hazlitt's.** This hotel, deep in the heart of Soho, is in three connected early 18th-century houses, one of which was the essayist William Hazlitt's (1778–1830) last home. It's an open secret that Hazlitt's is a disarmingly friendly place, full of personality. Robust antiques are everywhere, assorted prints crowd every wall, plants and stone sculptures (by one of the owners' father-in-law) appear in odd corners, and every room has a Victorian claw-foot bath in its bathroom. There are a tiny sitting room, wooden staircases, and more restaurants within strolling distance than you could patronize in a year. Book way ahead—this is the London address of media people and antique dealers everywhere. *6 Frith St., W1V 5TZ, tel. 071/434–1771, fax 071/439–1524. 23 rooms with bath. AE, DC, MC, V.*

Kensington

Very Expensive
★ **Blakes.** Blakes is another world—some would say a time-warp. It was designed by owner Anouska Hempel (aka Lady Weinberg), and each room is a fantasy packed with precious Biedermeier, Murano glass, and modern pieces inside walls of red lacquer and black, or dove-gray, or perhaps—like 007, the movie stars' favorite suite—pink. Moody lighting, including recessed spotlights, compounds the impression that you, too, are a movie star living in a big-budget biopic. The foyer sets the tone with its piles of cushions, Phileas Fogg valises and trunks, black walls, rattan and bamboo, and a noisy parakeet under a gigantic Asian parasol. Downstairs, an equally dramatic black-and-white restaurant displays Thai warriors' costumes in glass cases. Stay away if you don't like Hollywood or the music biz. *33 Roland Gdns., SW7 3PF, tel. 071/370–6701, fax 071/373–0442. 52 rooms with bath. Facilities: restaurant, satellite TV. AE, DC, MC, V.*

Expensive
★ **The Gore.** Just down the road from the Albert Hall, this small, very friendly hotel is run by the same people who run Hazlitt's (*see above*) and

features a similar eclectic selection of prints, etchings, and antiques. Here, though, are spectacular folly-like rooms—Room 101 is a Tudor fantasy with minstrel gallery, stained glass, and four-poster bed, and Room 211, done in over-the-top Hollywood style, has a tiled mural of Greek goddesses in the bathroom. Despite all that, the Gore manages to remain most elegant. Bistrot 190 (*see* Chapter 4, Dining) serves as dining rooms and bar. *189 Queen's Gate, SW7 5EX, tel. 071/584–6601, fax 071/589–8127. 54 rooms with bath. Facilities: brasserie restaurant, lounge. AE, DC, MC, V.*

Moderate **Kensington Close.** This large, fairly utilitarian hotel feels like a smaller one and boasts a few extras you wouldn't expect for the reasonable rate and convenient location (in a quiet lane off Kensington High Street). The main attraction is the health club, with an 18-meter pool, two squash courts, and a beauty salon; there's also a secluded little water garden. Standard rooms are on the small side, with plain chain-hotel (this one has belonged to the British Forte Hotels for 50 years) built-in furniture. Some Executive rooms are twice the size. Good value. *Wrights La., W8 5SP, tel. 071/937–8170, fax 071/937–8289. 530 rooms with bath. Facilities: 2 restaurants, 2 bars, lounge, garden, health club with indoor pool, satellite TV, baby-sitting. AE, DC, MC, V.*

Inexpensive **Clearlake.** A small hotel that also offers a few self-catering apartments. Rooms are cozy, with refrigerators, ample storage space, and huge windows. It is family-owned and -run. *19 Prince of Wales Ter., W8 5PQ, tel. 071/937–3274, fax 071/376–0604. 13 rooms with bath, 4 apartments. Facilities: baby-sitting, bar. AE, DC, MC, V.*

★ **Vicarage.** Family-owned for nearly 30 years, the Vicarage feels like a real home. It's beautifully decorated, in a quiet location overlooking a magnificent garden square and close to the Kensington shops. *10 Vicarage Gate, W8 4AG, tel. 071/229–4030. 19 rooms without bath. Facilities: lounge. No credit cards.*

Lodging in Kensington, Knightsbridge, Chelsea,

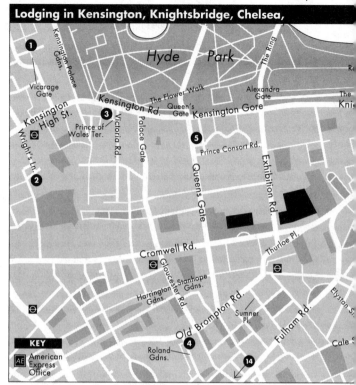

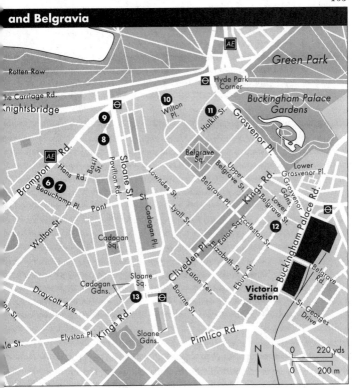

Knightsbridge, Chelsea, and Belgravia

Very Expensive ★   **Berkeley.** The Berkeley is a remarkably successful mixture of the old and the new. It is a luxurious, air-conditioned, double-glazed modern building with a splendid penthouse swimming pool that opens to the sky when the weather's good. The bedrooms are decorated by various designers, but tend to be serious and opulent, some with swags of William Morris prints, others plain and masculine with little balconies overlooking the street. All have sitting areas and big, tiled bathrooms with bidets. For the ridiculously rich, there are spectacular suites, one with its own conservatory terrace, another with a sauna, but—such is the elegance of this place—you'd feel almost as spoiled in a normal room. There's a rather good French restaurant (simply called the Berkeley Restaurant), as well as the Buttery, which serves light Mediterranean food, and the Oriental, tiered Perroquet bar, offering 52 cocktails until the early morning. The hotel is conveniently placed for Knightsbridge shopping. *Wilton Pl., SW1X 7RL, tel. 071/235–6000, fax 071/235–4330. 160 rooms with bath. Facilities: rooftop heated indoor and outdoor pool, gymnasium, massage, sauna, hairdressing, movie theater, florist, 2 restaurants. AE, DC, MC, V.*

★   **The Halkin.** This luxurious little place is looking even more different from the norm than it did last year. You could say its slickness doesn't belong in the '90s, or you could just enjoy the Milanese design: the clean-cut white marble lobby with its royal blue leather bucket chairs, the arresting curved charcoal-gray corridors, the "diseased mahogany" veneers that darken as you climb, and the gray-on-gray bedrooms that light up when you insert your electronic key. Wealthy business and media types frequent the Halkin, and they can't breathe easy without a fax, Reuters, and two phone lines with conference-call. These are provided, along with two touch-control pads for all the gadgets, cable TV and video (library downstairs), room safe, and minibar. The bathrooms are palaces of shiny chrome, anti-mist mirrors, and marble that changes color according to which of the elements your floor echoes. It might be like living

American Express offers Travelers Cheques built for two.

American Express® Cheques *for Two*. The first Travelers Cheques that allow either of you to use them because both of you have signed them. And only one of you needs to be present to purchase them.

Cheques *for Two* are accepted anywhere regular American Express Travelers Cheques are, which is just about everywhere. So stop by your bank, AAA* or any American Express Travel Service Office and ask for Cheques *for Two*.

AMERICAN EXPRESS · Travelers Cheques

in the Design Museum, except that this place
employs some of the friendliest staff around—
and they look pretty good in their white Armani
uniforms, too. Gualtiero Marchesi, the pricey
Italian restaurant overlooking a little garden,
often seems to be shut. *Halkin St., SW1X 7DJ,
tel. 071/333–1000, fax 071/333–1100. 41 rooms
with bath. Facilities: restaurant, cable TV, video library, personal faxes on request, Reuters
news service. AE, DC, MC, V.*

Expensive **Beaufort.** You can practically hear the jingle of
★ Harrods' cash registers from a room at the
Beaufort, the brainchild of ex–TV announcer
Diana Wallis, who employs an all-woman team to
run the hotel. Actually, "hotel" is a misnomer
for this elegant pair of Victorian houses. There's
a sitting room instead of Reception; guests have
a front door key and the run of the drinks cabinet. The high-ceilinged, generously propor-
tioned rooms are decorated in muted,
sophisticated shades to suit the muted, sophisticated atmosphere—but don't worry, you're encouraged by the incredibly sweet staff to feel at
home. The rates are higher than the top range
for this category but include unlimited drinks,
breakfast, plus membership at a local health
club. *33 Beaufort Gdns., SW3 1PP, tel. 071/584–
5252, fax 071/589–2834. 29 rooms with bath. Facilities: 24-hr. complimentary bar in the sitting
room, air-conditioning, video library, access to
nearby health club with pool. AE, DC, MC, V.*

★ **Eleven Cadogan Gardens.** This aristocratic,
late-Victorian gabled town house is the perfect
spot for a pampered honeymoon, but very difficult to get into—and we're not referring to the
lack of a sign or a reception desk. Fine period
furniture and antiques, books, and magazines
on the tables, landscape paintings and portraits, coupled with some of that solid, no-non-
sense furniture that *real* English country
houses have in unaesthetic abundance makes for
a family home ambience; you might be borrow-
ing the house and servants of some wealthy
friends while they're away. Take the elevator or
walk up the fine oak staircase to your room,
which will have mahogany furniture, a restful
color scheme, and pretty bedspreads and
drapes. The best rooms are at the back. There's

a private garden for use in warm weather. *11 Cadogan Gdns., Sloane Sq., SW3 2RJ, tel. 071/ 730–3426, fax 071/730–5217. 62 rooms with bath. Facilities: garden, chauffeur-driven car. No credit cards.*

★ **L'Hotel.** An upscale bed-and-breakfast run by the same Levins who own the Capital next door. This is a plainer alternative—less pampering, unfussy decor. There's an air of provincial France around, with the white wrought-iron bedsteads, pine furniture, and delicious breakfast croissants and baguettes (included in the room rate) served on that chunky dark green and gold Parisian café china in Le Metro cellar wine bar (also open to nonresidents). This really is like a house—you're given your own front door key, there's no elevator, and the staff leaves in the evening. Reserve ahead—it's very popular. *28 Basil St., SW3 1AT, tel. 071/589– 6286, fax 071/225–0011. 12 rooms with bath. Facilities: wine bar, restaurant. AE, V.*

Moderate **Basil Street.** Automatic membership for female ★ guests at the ladies' club here—the Parrot Club. The Basil Street is a gracious Edwardian hotel on a quiet street behind busy Brompton Road and off (rich) shoppers heaven, Sloane Street. It's been family-run for three quarters of a century. The upstairs lounge is a peaceful spot for coffee, drinks, or afternoon tea. All the bedrooms are different; many are like grandma's guest room, with overstuffed counterpanes and a random selection of furniture— some good pieces, some utilitarian. You can write letters home in the peaceful gallery, which has polished wooden floors and fine Turkish carpets underneath a higgledy-piggledy wealth of antiques. This is a very popular hotel among Americans with a taste for period charm, some of whom come back often enough to merit the title "Basilite"—a priveleged regular offered a 15% discount. *Basil St., SW3 1AH, tel. 071/581–3311, fax 071/581–3693. 92 rooms, 72 with bath. Facilities: wine bar, lounge, ladies' club, restaurant. AE, DC, MC, V.*

Claverley. Can't afford the Beaufort, but like the area? This B&B is on the same quiet street a moment from Harrods and makes a good alternative. The less expensive rooms have either bath or shower (not both); as you go up the scale, rooms get larger, decor (homey florals, either Victorian- or Edwardian-style) newer, and bathrooms better equipped; some top-rate rooms have four-poster beds. The service is friendly, everything's spotless, and breakfast is included. *13–14 Beaufort Gdns., SW3 1PS, tel. 071/589–8541, fax 071/584–3410. 36 rooms with bath. AE, V.*

Ebury Court. Here five 19th-century houses have been converted into an old-fashioned, family-run hotel close to Victoria Station. The rooms are smallish, with antique furniture to give them extra character—one of them has a grandfather clock and a Hepplewhite four-poster bed. The reception area, lounge, and restaurant are all freshly renovated, as are many of the bedrooms; some new ones were added recently, but some of them still have no bathroom. Be warned: Since the rates went up these are the only "moderate" rooms. *26 Ebury St., SW1W 0LU, tel. 071/730–8147, fax 071/823–5966. 45 rooms, 36 with bath. Facilities: bar, restaurant. MC, V.*

La Reserve. You'll find this unique small hotel in the lively, classy residential neighborhood of Fulham. The varnished floorboards, black venetian blinds, works of art (for sale), and primary-colored upholstery in the public areas are contemporary and sophisticated. Bedrooms are cluttered only with the minibars, hairdryers, trouser presses, and tea/coffee makers of more expensive places. It's a two-minute walk from Fulham Broadway tube, near Chelsea Football (soccer) Grounds and plenty of restaurants; there's also a brasserie in-house. *422–428 Fulham Rd., SW6 1DU, tel. 071/385–8561, fax 071/385–7662. 37 rooms with bath. Facilities: restaurant, bar, lounge, satellite TV. AE, DC, MC, V.*

Bayswater and Notting Hill Gate

Very Expensive **Halcyon.** It certainly is expensive, but you're paying for one of London's best small hotels. It was converted from two enormous wedding cake town houses just off Holland Park Avenue, which looks like a Parisian boulevard lined with mansions and plane trees and runs through this

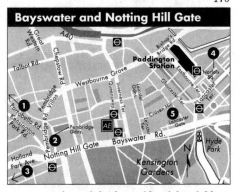

Bayswater and Notting Hill Gate

very upscale and leafy residential neighborhood. Elegance, space, and taste are unavoidable once you're through the doors here and the uniformed staff starts catering to your every whim. Each room has been designed separately; some have four-poster beds, others Jacuzzis. There's a stunning patio garden and a not-too-formal restaurant, The Room at the Halcyon. *81 Holland Park, W11 3RZ, tel. 071/727-7288, fax 071/229-8516. 44 rooms with bath. Facilities: restaurant, patio. AE, DC, MC, V.*

Expensive **Abbey Court.** Another very elegant little hotel
★ that is more like a private home—albeit one with a resident designer. It's in one of the gracious white Victorian mansions typical of this quiet, expensive neighborhood. Inside, that era is reflected in deep red wallpapers (downstairs), Murano glass and gilt-framed mirrors, framed prints, mahogany, and plenty of antiques. Bathrooms look the part but are entirely modern in gray Italian marble, with brass fittings and whirlpool baths. There's 24-hour room service instead of a restaurant (there are plenty around here, though), and guests can relax in the lounge or the pretty conservatory. *20 Pembridge Gdns., W2 4DU, tel. 071/221-7518, fax 071/792-0858. 22 rooms with bath. Facilities: Jacuzzis, conservatory, drawing room. AE, DC, MC, V.*

Moderate **Camelot.** Top marks to this affordable hotel,
★ with its freshly decorated bedrooms (featuring utility pine furniture, TVs, and tea/coffee mak-

ers) and attractive bathrooms. A full English breakfast is included in the room rate, which you eat in a very pretty breakfast room complete with exposed brick wall, large open fireplace, wooden farmhouse tables and floorboards, and a gallery of child guests' works of art. Everyone here is friendly beyond the call of duty. The few bathless single rooms are great bargains; ask also about the 10% discount for prepaid bookings of more than four nights. *45–47 Norfolk Sq., W2 1RX, tel. 071/723–9118, fax 071/402–3412. 34 rooms, 28 with bath. Facilities: free in-house videos, lounge. MC, V.*

★ **Portobello.** This small, eccentric hotel consists of two adjoining Victorian houses which (as is common around here) back onto a beautiful large garden that is shared with the neighbors. It has long been the favorite of the arty end of the music biz and other media types. Some rooms are minute, others huge—you must book well ahead or depend on luck. Big mirrors, palms, and ferns are everywhere, as befits the fantasy Victorian decor. The naughty round-bedded suite is popular. The basement bar/restaurant is one of many hangouts for locals in this very happening area. *22 Stanley Gdns., W11 2NG, tel. 071/727–2777, fax 071/792–9641. 25 rooms with bath. Facilities: bar, restaurant. AE, DC, MC, V. Closed 10 days over Christmas.*

Inexpensive **Lancaster Hall Hotel.** This modest hotel is owned by the German YMCA, which guarantees efficiency and spotlessness. There's a bargain 20-room "youth annex" offering basic rooms with shared baths. *35 Craven Terr., W2, tel. 071/723–9276, fax 071/224–8343. 100 rooms, 80 with bath or shower. Facilities: restaurant, bar. MC, V.*

Bloomsbury

Moderate **Whitehall.** An imposing entrance promises good things, which the interior more than lives up to. There's an elegant lobby with arched windows, and a garden bar leading onto a patio and not-too-manicured garden. A fine dining room offers both Continental and English breakfast, which is included in the (very moderate) rate. *2–5 Montague St., WC1B 5BU, tel. 071/580–5871,*

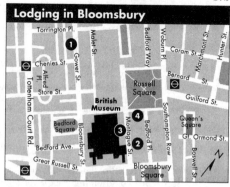

Lodging in Bloomsbury

fax 071/323–0409. 80 rooms, 20 with bath. Facilities: bar, restaurant. AE, DC, MC, V.

Inexpensive **Ridgemount.** The kindly owners, Mr. and Mrs.
★ Rees, make you feel at home. The public areas, especially the family-style breakfast room, have a friendly, cluttered Victorian feel. Some rooms overlook a leafy garden. *65 Gower St., WC1E 6HJ, tel. 071/636–1141. 15 rooms, none with bath. Facilities: lounge. No credit cards.*

Ruskin. Immediately opposite the British Museum, the family-owned Ruskin is both pleasant and quiet—all front windows are double-glazed. The bedrooms are clean, though nondescript; the back ones overlook a pretty garden. Note the bucolic mural (c. 1808) in the lounge. Well-run and very popular. *23–24 Montague St., WC1B 5BN, tel. 071/636–7388, fax 071/323–1662. 35 rooms, 7 with shower. Facilities: lounge. AE, DC, MC, V.*

St. Margaret's. This guest house on a tree-lined Georgian street has been run for many years by a friendly Italian family. You'll find spacious rooms and towering ceilings, and a wonderful location close to Russell Square. The back rooms have a garden view. *24 Bedford Pl., WC1B 5JL, tel. 071/636–4277. 64 rooms, 10 with bath. Facilities: 2 lounges. No credit cards.*

6 The Arts and Nightlife

The Arts

To find out what's on, check the extensive listings in the weekly magazine *Time Out*, which also prints reviews, or pick up the free fortnightly *London Theatre Guide* from cinemas and theaters, bookshops, cafés, and so forth. The *Evening Standard* also carries listings, especially the Friday edition, as do the "quality" Sunday papers and the Friday and Saturday *Independent*, *Guardian*, and *Times*. You'll find a rack overflowing with leaflets and flyers in most cinema and theater foyers, too.

Theater Of the 100 or so legitimate theaters in the capital, only about 30 are "West End," while the remainder go under the blanket title of "Fringe." Most theaters have matinees twice a week (Wednesday or Thursday and Saturday) and evening performances that begin at 7:30 or 8; performances on Sunday are rare. Prices vary, but in the West End you should expect to pay from £6 for a seat in the upper balcony to at least £20 for a good one in the stalls (orchestra) or dress circle (mezzanine). Tickets may be booked at the individual theater box offices, over the phone by credit card (some box offices or agents have special numbers for these marked "cc" in the phone book), or through ticket agents such as **First Call** (tel. 071/497–9977) or **Ticketmaster** (tel. 071/344–0055). If you're coming from the United States and wish to book seats in advance, **Keith Prowse** has a New York office (234 W. 44th St., Suite 1000, New York, NY 10036, tel. 212/398–1430 or 800/669–8687). Alternatively, the ticket booth (no telephone) on the southwest corner of Leicester Square sells half-price tickets on the day of performance for approximately 45 theaters (subject to availability). It's open Monday–Saturday 12–2 for matinees and 2:30–6:30 for evening performances; there is a £1.50 service charge, and only cash is accepted. All the larger hotels offer theater bookings, but as they tack on a hefty service charge, you would do better visiting the box offices yourself. You might, however, consider using one particular booking line that doubles the price of tickets: **West End Cares** (tel.

071/867–1111) donates half of what it charges to AIDS charities.

Warning: Be *very* careful of scalpers outside theaters; they have been known to charge £200 or more for a sought-after ticket. If you buy from such scalpers, you could easily end up with a forged ticket.

West End The **Royal Shakespeare Company** and the **Royal National Theatre Company** perform at London's two main arts complexes, the **Barbican Centre** (Barbican, EC2Y 8DS, tel. 071/638–8891) and **The National Theatre** (South Bank Arts Complex, SE1 9PX, tel. 071/928–2252) respectively. Both companies mount consistently excellent productions and are usually a safe option for anyone having trouble choosing which play to see.

Fringe Shows can be straight plays, circus, comedy, musicals, readings, or productions every bit as polished and impressive as those in the West End—except for their location and the price of the seat. Fringe tickets are always considerably less expensive than tickets for West End productions.

Concerts The ticket prices to symphony-size orchestral concerts are fortunately still relatively moderate, usually ranging from £5 to £15. If you can't book in advance, then arrive at the hall an hour before the performance for a chance at returns.

The London Symphony Orchestra is in residence at the **Barbican Arts Centre** (Barbican, EC2Y 8DS, tel. 071/638–8891 reservations or 071/638–4141 information) although other top orchestras—including the Philharmonia and the Royal Philharmonic—also perform here. The **South Bank Arts Complex** (South Bank, SE1 8XX, tel. 071/928–8800 reservations or 071/928–3002 information), which includes the **Royal Festival Hall,** the **Queen Elizabeth Hall,** and the small **Purcell Room,** forms another major venue; the Royal Festival Hall is one of the finest concert halls in Europe. For a different concert-going experience, as well as the chance to take part in a great British tradition, try the **Royal Albert Hall** (Kensington Gore, SW7 2AP, tel. 071/589–8212) during the Promenade Concert

West End Theaters and Concert Halls

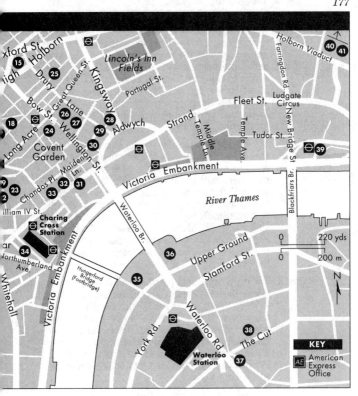

xford St.
igh Holborn
Holborn

15

Drury

Bow St.

Great Queen St.

25

26 **27**

Kingsway

Lincoln's Inn
Fields

Portugal St.

Fleet St.

Holborn Viaduct

40 **41**

Farringdon Rd.

Ludgate
Circus

New Bridge St.

18

24

Long Acre

Covent
Garden

Wellington St.

28

Aldwych

29

30

Strand

Middle
Temple Ln.

Temple Ave.

Tudor St.

39

Maiden Ln.

9
23
2

Chandos Pl.

33

32 **31**

Victoria Embankment

River Thames

Blackfriars Br.

illiam IV St.

**Charing
Cross
Station**

Northumberland
Ave.

Victoria Embankment

Waterloo Br.

34

ar

Whitehall

Hungerford
Bridge
(Footbridge)

35

36

Upper Ground

Stamford St.

0   220 yds

0   200 m

N

York Rd.

Waterloo Rd

The Cut

38

37

**Waterloo
Station**

KEY

AE   American
Express
Office

season: eight weeks lasting from July to September. Special "promenade" (standing) tickets usually cost half the price of normal tickets and are available at the hall on the night of the concert. Another summer pleasure is the outdoor concert series by the lake at **Kenwood** (Hampstead Heath; tel. 081/348–6684). Concerts are also part of the program at the open-air theater in **Holland Park** (no phone). Check the listings for details.

You should also look for the lunchtime concerts that take place all over the city in smaller concert halls, the big arts center foyers, and churches; they usually cost under £5 or are free and will feature string quartets, singers, jazz ensembles, or gospel choirs. **St. John's, Smith Square** (Smith Sq., SW1P 3HA, tel. 071/222–1061) and **St. Martin-in-the-Fields** (Trafalgar Sq., WC2N 4JJ, tel. 071/839–1930) are two of the more popular locations. Performances usually begin about 1 PM and last an hour.

Opera The main venue for opera in London is the **Royal Opera House** (Covent Garden, WC2E 9DD, tel. 071/240–1066), which ranks with the Metropolitan Opera House in New York—particularly where expense is concerned. Prices range from £5 in the upper slips (whether the stage is visible is anyone's guess) to £124 for the best seat. Performances are divided into booking periods and sell out early.

English-language productions are staged at the **Coliseum** (St. Martin's La., WC2N 4ES, tel. 071/836–3161), home of the English National Opera Company. Prices here are generally lower than at the Royal Opera House, ranging from £8 to £43, and productions are often innovative and exciting. The occasional megaproduction with international stars (plus live elephants and herds of horses) is staged at the **Wembley Arena**.

Ballet The Royal Opera House is also the home of the world-famous **Royal Ballet**. Prices are slightly more reasonable for the ballet than they are for the opera, but bookings should be made well in advance, as tickets sell out fast. The **English National Ballet** and visiting international companies perform at the Coliseum and the Royal Festival Hall from time to time. The **London**

City Ballet is based at **Sadler's Wells Theatre,** which also hosts various other ballet companies and regional and international modern dance troupes. Prices here are much cheaper than at Covent Garden.

Dance In addition to the many Fringe theaters that mount the odd dance performance, the following theaters showcase contemporary dance: **The Place** (17 Duke's Rd., WC1, tel. 071/387–0031); **Riverside Studios** (Crisp Rd., W69RL, tel. 081/748–3354); and **Sadler's Wells** (Rosebery Ave., EC1R 4TN, tel. 071/278–8916).

Movies Most of the major houses (Odeon, MGM, etc.) congregate in the Leicester Square/Piccadilly Circus area, where tickets average £4–£7, sometimes even more. Mondays and matinees are sometimes better buys at £2 to £4, and there are also fewer crowds.

Movie clubs and repertory cinemas screen a wider range of movies, including classics, Continental, and underground, as well as rare or underestimated masterpieces. Some charge a membership fee of under £1. One of the best is the **National Film Theatre** (in the South Bank Arts Complex; tel. 071/928–3232), where the London Film Festival is based in the fall. Daily memberships cost 40p. The **Institute of Contemporary Arts** (the Mall, tel. 071/930–3647) contains two cinemas (one is tiny).

Nightlife

Jazz **Bass Clef.** Owned by the delightful Peter Ind (himself a jazz bass player), this Bohemian backstreet club offers some of the best live jazz in London, along with fried chicken and burgers on weekends, snacks the rest of the time. Although it is difficult to see the stage from the tables, except from closed circuit screens, and it does get very full, warm, and smoky here, there is no problem with the acoustics. Music also at the adjoining **Tenor Clef** (1 Hoxton Sq.). *35 Coronet St., N1, tel. 071/729–2440/2476. Admission: £3.50–£7, depending on the band. Open Mon., Wed.–Sat. 7:30 PM–2 AM. AE, DC, MC, V.*

Jazz Cafe. This palace of high-tech cool in a converted bank in bohemian Camden has its problems—you often have to stand in line, and there never seems to be enough seating—but still it remains an essential hangout for fans of the mainstream end of the repertoire. Varied line-ups of international musicians, free Saturday lunchtime jazz, and good food make the (easy) journey north worthwhile. *5–7 Pkwy., NW1, tel. 071/916–6000 or 071/284–4358. Admission: £6–£10, depending on the band; £1 Sun. lunch. Open 7 PM–late (time varies) daily; noon–4 PM Sat., Sun. Reservations advised for balcony restaurant. AE, DC, MC, V.*

Ronnie Scott's. The legendary Soho jazz club which, since its opening in the early '60s, has been attracting all the big names. It's usually packed and hot, the food isn't great, service is slow—because the staff can't move through the crowds, either—but the atmosphere can't be beat, and it's probably still London's best. *47 Frith St., W1, tel. 071/439–0747. Admission £10–£12 non-members. Open Mon.–Sat. 8:30 PM–3 AM, Sun. 8 PM–11:30 PM. Reservations advised; essential some nights. AE, DC, MC, V.*

Music gigs in London are listed in full in *Time Out*, available from most newsdealers.

Nightclubs **Legends.** Revamped with an impressive high-tech interior designed by Eva Jiricna, this sleek club attracts a different age-range and style of clientele according to the night, but it tends to be full of the non-extreme type of regular "clubber"—youth that spends every spare penny on never staying in. Downstairs is a large, cool dance floor with a central bar. *29–30 Old Burlington St., W1, tel. 071/437–9933. Admission: Mon.–Thurs. £6 after 10 PM; Fri.–Sat. £8 after 10 PM. Open Mon.–Sat. 9 PM–3 AM. Dress: stylish. AE, DC, MC, V.*

Palookaville. Conveniently close to Covent Garden tube, this basement restaurant/bar charges a cover only on Friday and Saturday. It's popular with office people for after-hours drinks. You won't write home about the food or the undemanding music—usually there's a jazz trio or similar live band—but you might about the friendly, mellow ambience. *13A James St., WC2, tel. 071/240–5857. Admission: £3 Fri., Sat. Open Mon.–Thurs. 8:30–midnight, Fri. and Sat. 8:30–1. AE, DC, MC, V.*

Stringfellows. Peter Stringfellow's first London nightclub opened ten years ago and remains a glitzy locale. Art deco motifs decorate the upstairs restaurant, with prices from £30. Mirrored walls and a heady light show set the tempo on the downstairs dance floor. *16–19 Upper St. Martin's La., WC2, tel. 071/240–5534. Admission: Mon.–Wed. £8; Thurs. £10; Fri.–Sat. before 10, £10, after 10, £15. Open Mon.–Sat. 8 PM–3:30 AM. Dress: stylish. AE, DC, MC, V.*

Discos   **Café de Paris.** This former gilt and red velveteen ballroom still looks like a disreputable teadance hall but hosts fun nights for 20-to-30-somethings who dress the part. At press time, Wednesdays were for a slightly older crowd; Fridays were called **Sex.** But ring for current details. *3 Coventry St., W1, tel. 071/287–3602. Admission: £5–£12. Open. Wed. 10 PM–4 AM, Thurs.–Sat. 11 PM–6 AM. Dress: trendy. No credit cards.*

Camden Palace. The jeunesse crowd is attracted by the famous "theme nights," the fast-food–style restaurant, and the cocktail bar where you can order anything from Between The Sheets to a Slow Comfortable Screw. The large central disco features nonstop laser light shows. *1A Camden High St., NW1, tel. 071/387–0428. Admission: £3–£9. Open Tues.–Sat. 9 PM–3 AM. Dress: casual stylish.*

Heaven. London's premier (mainly) gay club is the best place for dancing wildly for hours. A state-of-the-art laser show and a large, throbbing dance floor complement a labyrinth of quieter bars and lounges and a snack bar. *Under the Arches, Craven St., WC2, tel. 071/839–3852. Admission: £2–£8 depending on night. Call for opening times (approx. 10 PM–3 AM). Dress: stylish casual. MC, V.*

Casinos   The 1968 Gaming Act states that any person wishing to gamble *must* make a declaration of intent to gamble at the gaming house in question and *must* apply for membership in person. Membership usually takes about two days. In many cases, clubs prefer for the applicant's membership to be proposed by an existing member. Personal guests of existing members are, however, allowed to participate.

Crockford's. This is a civilized club, established 150 years ago, with none of the jostling for tables that mars many of the flashier clubs. It has attracted a large international clientele since its move from St. James's to Mayfair. The club offers American roulette, Punto Banco, and blackjack. *30 Curzon St., W1, tel. 071/493–7771. Membership £150 a year. Open daily 2 PM–4 AM. Jacket and tie required.*

Sportsman Club. One of the few casinos in London to have a dice table as well as Punto Banco, American roulette, and blackjack. *3 Tottenham Court Rd., W1, tel. 071/637–5464. Membership £3.45 a year. Open daily 2 PM–4 AM. Jacket and tie required.*

Rock   **The Forum.** The former Town & Country, this ex-ballroom with balcony and dance floor packs in the customers and consistently attracts the best medium-to-big-name performers, too. At press time plans were in the works for a West End branch. *9–17 Highgate Rd., NW5, tel. 071/ 284–0303. Admission: around £8–£12. Open most nights 7–11. Dress: youth/casual.*

100 Club. Originally renowned as a place for traditional jazz (still played on Wednesday and Saturday), there's a more varied music menu nowadays, though you're more likely to find blues than thrash metal. Fast food is sometimes available. *100 Oxford St., W1, tel. 071/636– 0933. Admission: £3–£6, depending on band. Open Mon.–Sat. 7:45 PM–1, Sun. 7:45 PM– 11:30.*

The Rock Garden. Famous for the setting and for encouraging young talent to move on to bigger and better things. Talking Heads, U2, and The Smiths are just a few who made their debuts here. Music is in the basement, where there is standing room only, so it is advisable to eat first. *6–7 The Piazza, Covent Gdn., WC2, tel. 071/ 240–3961. Admission: £4–£7 depending on band. Open Mon.–Sat. 7:30 PM–3 AM; Sun. 8 PM–midnight. AE, DC, MC, V.*

Weekly events are listed in *Time Out* or in one of the rock magazines such as *New Musical Express, Melody Maker,* or *Sounds,* available every Thursday.

Index

Personal Itinerary

Departure *Date*

Time

Transportation

Arrival *Date*   *Time*

Departure *Date*   *Time*

Transportation

Arrival *Date*   *Time*

Departure *Date*   *Time*

Transportation

Arrival *Date*   *Time*

Departure *Date*   *Time*

Transportation

Personal Itinerary

Arrival *Date*   *Time*

Departure *Date*   *Time*

Transportation

Arrival *Date*   *Time*

Departure *Date*   *Time*

Transportation

Arrival *Date*   *Time*

Departure *Date*   *Time*

Transportation

Arrival *Date*   *Time*

Departure *Date*   *Time*

Transportation

Addresses

Name	*Name*
Address	*Address*
Telephone	*Telephone*
Name	*Name*
Address	*Address*
Telephone	*Telephone*
Name	*Name*
Address	*Address*
Telephone	*Telephone*
Name	*Name*
Address	*Address*
Telephone	*Telephone*
Name	*Name*
Address	*Address*
Telephone	*Telephone*
Name	*Name*
Address	*Address*
Telephone	*Telephone*
Name	*Name*
Address	*Address*
Telephone	*Telephone*
Name	*Name*
Address	*Address*
Telephone	*Telephone*

Fodor's Travel Guides

Available at bookstores everywhere, or call 1-800-533-6478, 24 hours a day.

U.S. Guides

Alaska

Arizona

Boston

California

Cape Cod, Martha's Vineyard, Nantucket

The Carolinas & the Georgia Coast

Chicago

Colorado

Florida

Hawaii

Las Vegas, Reno, Tahoe

Los Angeles

Maine, Vermont, New Hampshire

Maui

Miami & the Keys

New England

New Orleans

New York City

Pacific North Coast

Philadelphia & the Pennsylvania Dutch Country

The Rockies

San Diego

San Francisco

Santa Fe, Taos, Albuquerque

Seattle & Vancouver

The South

The U.S. & British Virgin Islands

The Upper Great Lakes Region

USA

Vacations in New York State

Vacations on the Jersey Shore

Virginia & Maryland

Waikiki

Walt Disney World and the Orlando Area

Washington, D.C.

Foreign Guides

Acapulco, Ixtapa, Zihuatanejo

Australia & New Zealand

Austria

The Bahamas

Baja & Mexico's Pacific Coast Resorts

Barbados

Berlin

Bermuda

Brazil

Brittany & Normandy

Budapest

Canada

Cancun, Cozumel, Yucatan Peninsula

Caribbean

China

Costa Rica, Belize, Guatemala

The Czech Republic & Slovakia

Eastern Europe

Egypt

Euro Disney

Europe

Europe's Great Cities

Florence & Tuscany

France

Germany

Great Britain

Greece

The Himalayan Countries

Hong Kong

India

Ireland

Israel

Italy

Japan

Kenya & Tanzania

Korea

London

Madrid & Barcelona

Mexico

Montreal & Quebec City

Morocco

Moscow & St. Petersburg

The Netherlands, Belgium & Luxembourg

New Zealand

Norway

Nova Scotia, Prince Edward Island & New Brunswick

Paris

Portugal

Provence & the Riviera

Rome

Russia & the Baltic Countries

Scandinavia

Scotland

Singapore

South America

Southeast Asia

Spain

Sweden

Switzerland

Thailand

Tokyo

Toronto

Turkey

Vienna & the Danube Valley

Yugoslavia

Special Series

Fodor's Affordables
Caribbean

Europe

Florida

France

Germany

Great Britain

London

Italy

Paris

Fodor's Bed & Breakfast and Country Inns Guides
Canada's Great Country Inns

California

Cottages, B&Bs and Country Inns of England and Wales

Mid-Atlantic Region

New England

The Pacific Northwest

The South

The Southwest

The Upper Great Lakes Region

The West Coast

The Berkeley Guides
California

Central America

Eastern Europe

France

Germany

Great Britain & Ireland

Mexico

Pacific Northwest & Alaska

San Francisco

Fodor's Exploring Guides
Australia

Britain

California

The Caribbean

Florida

France

Germany

Ireland

Italy

London

New York City

Paris

Rome

Singapore & Malaysia

Spain

Thailand

Fodor's Flashmaps
New York

Washington, D.C.

Fodor's Pocket Guides
Bahamas

Barbados

Jamaica

London

New York City

Paris

Puerto Rico

San Francisco

Washington, D.C.

Fodor's Sports
Cycling

Hiking

Running

Sailing

The Insider's Guide to the Best Canadian Skiing

Skiing in the USA & Canada

Fodor's Three-In-Ones (guidebook, language cassette, and phrase book)
France

Germany

Italy

Mexico

Spain

Fodor's Special-Interest Guides
Accessible USA

Cruises and Ports of Call

Euro Disney

Halliday's New England Food Explorer

Healthy Escapes

London Companion

Shadow Traffic's New York Shortcuts and Traffic Tips

Sunday in New York

Walt Disney World and the Orlando Area

Walt Disney World for Adults

Fodor's Touring Guides
Touring Europe

Touring USA: Eastern Edition

Fodor's Vacation Planners
Great American Vacations

National Parks of the East

National Parks of the West

The Wall Street Journal Guides to Business Travel
Europe

International Cities

Pacific Rim

USA & Canada

WHEREVER YOU TRAVEL, *H*ELP IS NEVER FAR AWAY.

From planning your trip to replacing
lost Cards, American Express® Travel Service
Offices* are always there to help.

LONDON

6 Haymarket
071-930-4411

78 Brompton Road
Knightsbridge
071-584-6182

54 Cannon Street
071-248-2671

4 Millbank
071-222-1500

89 Mount Street
071-499-4436

British Travel Centre
4-12 Lower Regent St.
071-839-2682

Debenhams
Oxford Street
071-408-3644

Halifax Building
Society
Whiteleys Centre,
Queensway
071-221-7190

134 Southampton
Row
071-837-4416

London House
213-233 Regent St.
071-499-6182

147 Victoria St.
071-828-7411

Wimbledon Travel Ltd.
85 High Street
Wimbledon Village
081-947-6281

**American Express Travel Service Offices are found in
central locations throughout the United Kingdom.**